INTERVIEW FOR SUCCESS

Books and CD-ROMs by Drs. Ron and Caryl Krannich

101 Dynamite Answers to Interview Questions
101 Secrets of Highly Effective Speakers
201 Dynamite Job Search Letters
Best Jobs For the 21st Century
Change Your Job, Change Your Life
The Complete Guide to International Jobs and Careers
The Complete Guide to Public Employment
The Directory of Federal Jobs and Employers
Discover the Best Jobs For You!
Dynamite Cover Letters
Dynamite Networking For Dynamite Jobs
Dynamite Résumés
Dynamite Salary Negotiations
Dynamite Tele-Search
The Educator's Guide to Alternative Jobs and Careers
Find a Federal Job Fast!
From Air Force Blue to Corporate Gray
From Army Green to Corporate Gray
From Navy Blue to Corporate Gray
High Impact Résumés and Letters
International Jobs Directory
Interview For Success
Job-Power Source CD-ROM
Jobs and Careers With Nonprofit Organizations
Jobs For People Who Love Travel
Mayors and Managers
Moving Out of Education
Moving Out of Government
The Politics of Family Planning Policy
Re-Careering in Turbulent Times
Résumés and Job Search Letters For Transitioning Military Personnel
Shopping and Traveling in Exotic Asia
Shopping in Exciting Australia and Papua New Guinea
Shopping in Exotic Places
Shopping the Exotic South Pacific
Treasures and Pleasures of Australia
Treasures and Pleasures of China
Treasures and Pleasures of Hong Kong
Treasures and Pleasures of Indonesia
Treasures and Pleasures of Italy
Treasures and Pleasures of Paris and the French Riviera
Treasures and Pleasures of Singapore and Malaysia
Treasures and Pleasures of Thailand
Ultimate Job Source CD-ROM

INTERVIEW FOR SUCCESS
A Practical Guide to Increasing
Job Interviews, Offers, and Salaries

Seventh Edition

Caryl Rae Krannich, Ph.D.
Ronald L.Krannich, Ph.D.

IMPACT PUBLICATIONS
Manassas Park, VA

❖ INTERVIEW FOR SUCCESS: A Practical Guide to ❖
Increasing Job Interviews, Offers, and Salaries

Seventh Edition

Dedicated to Marjorie Smith Woodring who instilled the values of education and perseverance imbued with the strength of love and support. With love and thanks from a grateful daughter.

Copyright © 1982, 1988, 1990, 1993, 1995, 1997, 1998 by Caryl Rae Krannich and Ronald L. Krannich

Library of Congress Cataloging-in-Publication Data

Krannich, Caryl Rae
    Interview for success : a practical guide to increasing job interviews, offers and salaries / Caryl Rae Krannich, Ronald L. Krannich.—7th ed.
    p. cm.
    ISBN 1-57023-098-6 (alk. paper)
    1. Employment interviewing. I. Krannich, Ronald L. II. Title.
HF5549.5.I6K72   1998
650.14—dc21   98-16136
                                 CIP

For information on distribution or quantity discount rates, call 703/361-7300 or write to: Sales Department, IMPACT PUBLICATIONS, 9104-N Manassas Drive, Manassas Park, VA 20111-5211, Tel. 703/361-7300, Fax 703/335-9486 or e-mail: impactp@impactpublications.com. Distributed to the trade by National Book Network, 15200 NBN Way, Blue Ridge Summit, PA 17214, Tel. 1-800-462-6420.

Contents

CHAPTER 4: Organize Your Job Search 31

CHAPTER 5: Encounter Different Interviews 44

CHAPTER 6: Network For Interviews 62

- Choose What's Best for You 183
- What You Get 184
- Process and Strategy Skills 185
- Specific Employment Fields 190
- Specialized Career Groups 191
- Bibliography 192

Preface

L anding a good job and advancing one's career as we move into the 21st century requires more than just responding to job vacancy announcements and waiting to be called for an interview. Increasingly job seekers must move from relatively passive job search activities to those involving greater initiative for uncovering job leads and scheduling interviews with prospective employers. This book is designed to assist you in moving to these active job search activities— getting and conducting interviews in today's job market.

We wrote this book because we saw a need for an interview book that would do seven things not found in most other interview books:

- Place the job interview within the larger career planning and job search **process** while, at the same time, deal with the **form, structure**, and **substance** of job interviews.

- Treat the interview as a **skill** that can be learned and applied with success.

- Specify how to **organize** oneself for getting, conducting, and following-up the interview.

- Treat the interview as a critical **communication process** involving both verbal and nonverbal communication as well as written and oral communication.

- Examine in how-to terms all of the critical **steps** in the interview process, from networking to writing thank you letters, and relate each step to one another.

- Offer **examples** and **dialogues** to illustrate important points rather than present them as "scripts" to be used in playing interview roles.

- Present a **complete**, **concise**, and **easy-to-use** guide to quickly prepare anyone for a job interview.

Above all, we saw a need for a separate book on the interview process developed around a clear concept of career development and the job search and designed to quickly move users from one interview step to another. We purposefully focus the interview in relation to other critical job search steps: identifying skills, stating objectives, writing resumes and letters, conducting research, and networking. To examine interviewing in isolation of these other job search activities would be a disservice. Indeed, we would neglect the key to effective interviewing—how well each job search activity relates to the final step—the interview which results in a job offer.

Interviewing is a skill you can learn. How effectively you learn and practice it is partly a function of how well your interview preparation is linked to the other job search steps.

Throughout this book we stress the importance of **communication** in the job search. The interview is communication. Its channels are letters, resumes, telephones, computers, and face-to-face meetings. Its goals, settings, formats, and techniques are varied. The sooner you recognize the interview as an important **verbal and nonverbal communication encounter**, the better you will present yourself in the job search. If employers—as they themselves indicate—want to know your strengths and value, then you must clearly communicate your strengths and value to them in the best manner possible.

We've attempted to craft an interview book that would be as complete, concise, and honest as possible. When addressing key elements in the interview process—especially interviewer-interviewee dialogues —we include the minimum amount of necessary how-to information without belaboring points or overwhelming you with exercises, examples, or illustrations. At no point do we suggest you arm yourself with someone else's "canned" answers to interview questions. To do so would be contrary to our notion of what you should be communicating in your job search—**your strengths and value**. Interviewing is not, and should never be, a game of acquiring and memorizing scripts for playing a role. Throughout your job search you must be honest with yourself and prospective employers. For how well you do in the interview merely sets the stage for how well you will do and how happy you will be on the job.

You should read this book at least a week or two before an interview to allow sufficient time to work through the strengths identification exercises and to anticipate questions and consider positive responses. However, should you be short on time—only a day or two until the interview—go directly to Chapter 3 as well as complete Chapters 7-13. Together these sections constitute a "crash course" on interviewing.

Most important, though, is how you use this book. Reading it is the first step. As with any how-to book, you must get **motivated** and **take action** to make it work for you. If you want to interview for success, you must carefully examine both **how** and **what** you will communicate to interviewers as well as make whatever changes are necessary to clearly communicate your strengths and value. If you do this, you will join thousands of others who each day successfully apply the strategies to interview for success!

Caryl Rae Krannich
Ronald L. Krannich

INTERVIEW FOR SUCCESS

1

Manage the Interview For Success

They just called. You've got a job interview for 9am on Monday! *"I don't believe it,"* you say. *"I thought this would never come. I've spent weeks responding to job listings, circulating my resume, writing letters, pounding the pavement, and receiving rejections as well as promising leads. This has not been my idea of a good time. But finally my job search has paid off. If I can just do well in the interview—be my very best self—I can get this job, make good money, and enjoy the good life. But what happens if I blow it? What can I do between now and Monday to prepare?"*

Success or Stress

Congratulations, you've got an interview. We hope you are on the way to a job that's right for you. You are wise to recognize the importance of the interview as well as to question what you can do to prepare. While that phone call is a sign of success, you still have hurdles to clear before you are offered the job. You need to prepare to interview for success rather than experience failure because you were unprepared.

Let's be perfectly clear about what that phone call means. You got the call and an invitation to interview **because** you were successful in marketing your resume, writing letters, and networking for job leads. After all, the specific goal of writing a resume, letters, and networking is to get a job interview—not a job. The invitation to interview appears to put you closer to an actual job, but it is not a job offer—only an invitation to ask you, in person, some questions to further determine your capabilities for a specific position as well as assess how well you might fit into the organization.

Remember, it's not over until you and the employer finalize the nuts-and-bolts of the employment process—a firm offer detailing your duties, responsibilities, and negotiation of your salary and benefits. These are the most desirable outcomes of the interview process. In fact, this could be one of many invitations to interview you receive on the road to getting the job you really want.

By the way, did you know you just had your first interview when you answered the phone and received the invitation to interview? That's right. You were most likely screened over the phone for what should become your next interview—a face-to-face meeting which is the formal job interview. Congratulations, you just came through your first interview with success!

> **The specific goal of writing a resume and letters and networking is to get a job interview—not a job.**

Even though you have learned a great deal about yourself and others during these past few weeks of job hunting, let's face it, you are not in this for the learning experience. Despite what all those career counselors and books say, finding a job is no fun. You put a lot of your ego on the line and risk rejection every time you make a phone call or send out a resume. Besides, you would rather be employed and making money—right?

Try as we may to make the job search process upbeat and positive, the job search process seems demeaning to many people. It seems so impersonal, superficial, and detached. It appears to be a game of chance where timing and luck often seem more important in the hiring process than one's hard-earned skills and capabilities. Employers quickly screen many people and then select a few for the final selection. They don't have or take time to really get to know you. While it may be a selection process for interviewers, it's an elimination game for interviewees.

You may have experienced weeks of mixed emotions. You've seen the peaks and valleys, and it may seem that the lows have been far more prevalent than the highs. After all, you have put your ego on the line, displayed your weaknesses to strangers, collected rejections, felt frustrated, developed false expectations, and experienced disappointments. Now you are supposed to put on your best performance as you walk on the employer's stage to clearly communicate—both verbally and non-verbally—why the employer should hire you. Now it's on to the interview where you will probably experience the greatest **stress** in all of your job search.

Old Adage Truths

Just how ready are you for this interview? Will you interview for success? What are you going to do between now and the interview on Monday? What questions will the interviewer most likely ask you? How will you answer them? Are there certain questions you may have trouble answering or which may reveal your weaknesses and thus disqualify you from further consideration? What additional information do you need about this employer? What questions should you ask during the interview? Is this the type of organization you really would like to work in? What will you do if you are offered a job? Are you prepared to accept the first offer presented to you or are you planning to negotiate the best possible salary?

Let's get even more specific. What are you going to wear on Monday—especially the colors, fabrics, and styles? What time will you arrive? What is the first thing you will do when you meet the interviewer face-to-face? Remember the old adage—**you never have a chance to make a second first impression**. And that is what the interview is all about—making good first impressions.

Better still, are you prepared to answer these basic knee benders?

- Why should I hire you?

- What are your weaknesses?

- What do you want to be doing five years from now?

- What are your salary expectations?

- Give me an example of a time when you made a bad decision.

Got some good answers? They better be good, because these are some of the most important questions interviewers pose either directly or indirectly.

Managing Stress to Your Advantage

We all want to be the very best we can. And if you will anticipate and prepare for the questions you can expect to be asked and fine tune your interpersonal and communication skills, you should do your best in the crucial job interview. That's what this book is all about—getting ready to do **your** very best.

While you are excited about getting a job, if you are like most people you will be apprehensive about the job interview. Your ego is on the line. You might succeed, yet you might fail. The interviewer will ask you many questions to determine whether you are the right person for the job. To communicate that you are the best, you must let the prospective employer know your strengths and value. Yes, you believe they should hire you rather than other candidates. But how can you best manage the interview so the interviewer shares this perception? What makes you so special in the eyes of the employer? Do you have something the others lack? Are you more capable, enthusiastic, or personable? Why should they think you are the best and hire you?

> **Let the prospective employer know your strengths and your value.**

If the thoughts of being subjected to numerous questions, closely scrutinized by employers, and possibly rejected are enough to make your throat dry and your palms sweat, you are not alone. Most people facing a prospective job interview experience some nervous apprehension and fear. While they know the interview is a critical step in getting a job, they prefer avoiding it altogether because of its possible negative consequence —a rejection.

The job interview is a different type of job search activity from writing letters, using the telephone, or meeting people for information, advice, and referrals. Analogous in some ways to trying out for a part in a theatrical performance, the job interview places you on center stage for a **part** in the employer's organization. Employers want the best for their money. Your actions—both verbal and nonverbal—should clearly communicate that **you** are the best one for the part.

Skills You Can Learn

This book is designed as a "hands-on" primer to quickly prepare you for the crucial job interview. We've eliminated much of the verbiage found in other interview books or in academic treatments of the subject so you can get right down to what is most important to know about each step in the interview process. If your interview is next week or even tomorrow, read Chapter 3, Chapters 7-12, and Appendix C immediately so you will know the basics for managing a successful interview.

We find it useful to view the job interview as a set of **verbal and nonverbal skills** that can be quickly learned. Our purposes are to show you how to minimize job interviewing stress, present your best self during the interview, and leave the interview with successful outcomes. Page after page outline the skills for managing the interview to your advantage. Upon completing this book you should be well prepared to conduct effective interviews that lead to the ultimate job search success—a job offer for a job that's right for you.

Interview Power

The job interview plays a powerful role in the screening and selection processes of employers as well as in your future career advancement. But exactly how important is it for both you and the employer? This question is best answered by addressing three additional questions on the role of job interviews.

1. How important is the interview in determining who is offered the job?

In study after study employers say the job interview is the single most important activity determining whom they hire. While grade point average, work experience, good recommendations, resumes, and networking are important concerns, they are of lesser importance than the actual face-to-face job interview. These other factors help get you invited to the interview. But the interview determines whether or not you get the job offer. Fail your interview and you're out of the hiring picture. Knowing this, you should spend a disproportionate amount of time preparing to do your very best in the job interview. Don't expect to walk into an interview and "just be yourself"; you must prepare to meet and exceed the expectations of what constitutes a "good interview" in the eyes of employers.

2. **Assuming you accept a job offer, how will the way you conduct the interview—especially salary negotiations—affect your future with the employer as well as your future salary levels?**

Employers agree the job interview is an important factor in determining how well an individual will be treated on the job in terms of both **respect and salary**. Haldane Associates, for example, note from years of experience with thousands of clients that *"Employees who have handled themselves well during their salary negotiations were treated with greater respect and were given more opportunities to advance within the organization."* Others agree with the importance of **how you conduct yourself in the interview**: you must be professional at all times, keeping in mind the interview leaves both a first and lasting impression from which employers develop expectations about how well you will fit into their organization. As for salary negotiations, remember a simple fact of economic life: the salary you negotiate establishes a **base** from which your future salaries with this as well as other employers will be influenced. Salary increments will most likely be figured as a percentage increase on this base. When you change jobs, your previous earnings will be one major basis for determining your new salary.

3. **How frequently will you face job interviews?**

In today's work world changing jobs and careers is a fact of life. Most people will have several jobs—perhaps a new job every two to three years—due to a combination of voluntary and forced job and career changes attendant with new technologies, recessions, terminations, and career advancements. While some of these new jobs will be found within one's present organization, most jobs will be in other organizations. In either case, each job change will require another round of job interviews. Since 95% of employers require interviews as part of their selection procedures—the percentage is even higher for managerial/professional positions—you can expect to participate in several job interviews in the years ahead. As your career advances, each interview will become even more important to your future career advancement and earnings.

Successful Outcomes

While job interviews are an important step to getting a job, the interview process can lead to several outcomes which may or may not be positive for you and your career. Therefore, it is important to clarify your goals prior to conducting a job interview. What, for example, do you want to accomplish in a job interview?

Most people still view interview success in narrow terms: success is to get a job offer. But to get the job offer is only one of many outcomes of the employment interview which may or may not be positive for you. Only time and experience on the job will tell you if getting the job was a good idea.

An important goal and outcome of any job interview should be to **obtain useful information** to determine whether the job is right for you. Success in the interview may mean learning that the position is **not** for you, and thus you turn down the job offer. Or perhaps the offer is not made since the interviewer also realizes the job is not a good fit for you. If you view a major goal of your interview to be gathering information, you will most likely perform better in the interview situation. Rather than feel you are in a stressful win-lose game, you will be more at ease as you focus on what the interview is all about—**an exchange of useful information between the interviewer and interviewee**. It is to your advantage to make sure this exchange takes place in your favor. You gain information about the job and present yourself, with honesty, in the most positive way possible.

Another successful outcome would be to market yourself for future positions in this or other organizations. The interview could establish a good basis for developing a job information and referral network.

As you use this book we urge you to approach the interview as a two-way street: both you and the employer want to better know each other. While the interviewer is trying to determine whether to hire you, you should be determining whether you want to work for the employer. There is nothing worse than dampening the euphoria of getting the job with the realization two months later that the job is not right for you. So beware of supposedly positive outcomes—job offers—that can lead to negative career experiences!

> **Success may mean learning the position is not for you.**

Use This Book For Success

We designed this book to best prepare you for the critical job interview. In each chapter we present practical how-to advice for effectively managing interviews for positive outcomes.

In Chapter 2 you'll have the opportunity to take an I.Q. test. No, it's not a test to determine your intelligence! In this case the "I.Q." stands for your "Interview Quotient'" which is a pretest to assess your present level of knowledge about the job interview. View this exercise as a chance to see how your views on the interview process compare with the advice of career specialists.

In Chapter 3 we identify 25 common myths associated with different steps in the job interview process. These myths may prevent you from becoming an effective interviewee. Therefore, we outline the corresponding realities for each myth. Taken together these myths and realities provide a brief overview of the major concerns in parparing for a managing an effective job interview.

In Chapter 4 we place the employment interview within the larger context of the job search process and offer useful advice for conducting an effective job search. By far the most important job search activity, the job interview is only one of several crucial steps in your overall job search. It cannot be dealt with in isolation of the other steps. Above all, the interview must be closely related to resume writing and networking.

In Chapter 5 we outline different types, settings, and formats of interviews you are most likely to encounter. These include informational/networking, screening, selection/hiring, series, panel, and stress interviews. They are conducted over the telephone or in face-to-face settings for both screening and hiring purposes.

In Chapters 6, 7, and 8 we examine strategies for getting informational and job interviews, acquiring information about employers, and preparing for the day of the interview. Here you will find several important interview "do's" and "don'ts" as well as sample questions which stress your strengths in contrast to the interviewer's desire to know your weaknesses.

In Chapters 9 and 10 we look at both verbal and nonverbal communication during the interview. We include several important "do's" and "don'ts" as well as sample questions which stress your strengths in contrast to the interviewer's desire to know your weaknesses.

Chapters 11 and 12 complete the most important steps in the job interview. In these chapters we focus on how to best negotiate salary, close the interview, and conduct interview follow-ups.

> **Good interviewing is based upon a strong job search foundation of self-assessment, skills identification, objective setting, research, resume and letter writing, and networking.**

At the very end of the book we include sample letters appropriate for different types of interviews, a listing of interview maxims for quickly reviewing the contents of the book, and a list of recommended interview and job search resources.

Three statements of caution are in order before we dive into the remainder of this book. First, if you have not done your homework by completing the other critical steps in the job search, we strongly urge you to begin now. The lesson we and others have learned over the years is this: good interviewing is based upon a strong job search foundation of self-assessment, skills identification, objective setting, research, resume and letter writing, and networking. Please don't short-change yourself by failing to do this homework.

Second, if you are in a real hurry—your interview is scheduled within the next 48 hours—you may wish to skip Chapters 4, 5, and 6. Start with the interviewing myths and realities in Chapter 3 and then go to Chapters 7 through 12 and Appendix C. These chapters take you directly into the interview. They should get you up and going within three hours. The first few chapters cover many of the basics you need to know prior to conducting the interview.

Third, time permitting, do complete the checklists and forms appearing in these chapters. They are designed to quickly generate important information you need for managing the interview.

Taken together, these chapters cover the major practical aspects of conducting effective job interviews within the framework of a well planned job search designed for the 21st century. If you follow the advice outlined in these chapters, you should lessen your fear and apprehension by taking better control of the interview situation. You will do what many other skilled job hunters are increasingly doing today—managing the interview to their advantage. In addition to generating more job offers, they have the advantage of knowing when to accept or reject job offers. Being selective individuals, they get jobs that are right for them.

Whether you are entering the job market for the first time or making a job or career change—forced or by choice—a job interview is almost certain to be a necessary and important step in landing a job. How you manage that interview will make a major difference in both your professional and personal lives.

So read on, for the rest of this book will show you what the interviewer really looks for and how you can prepare yourself to convey your strengths without letting your weaknesses mar the positive image you wish to project. In the end, you want nothing less than to interview for success!

Test Your I.Q. For Success

Y ou have probably taken several I.Q. tests during your years in school. Those were standardized tests designed to measure your intelligence. Our I.Q. test is designed to measure your Interview Quotient—your knowledge, skills, and abilities relevant to job interviews.

The questions posed in this chapter are designed to test not your basic intelligence, but to test your interview savvy. How well you prepare for the job interview as well as how you actually conduct yourself in the interview depends in part on your perceptions of the purpose of the interview as well as your notions of the goals of the interviewer and the interviewee. The greater the congruence of your expectations for this job interview and the reality of the situation, the more likely both you and the employer will leave the interview feeling good about what was accomplished.

So sharpen your pencil and get ready to see how you view the job interview. This will probably be the least stressful I.Q. test you have ever taken!

Identify Your Interview Quotient

Each of us has a capacity to do well in a job interview. Some people always seem to interview well. They have the personality, social graces, knowledge, and experience that impresses potential employers. Others are not so fortunate. Finding the job interview an extremely stressful situation, they need tips on what they should know and how they should best prepare for the interview. They find job search and interview books, such as this one, useful in their preparation.

Complete the following exercise by indicating your degree of agreement or disagreement with each statement by circling the number to the right that best represents your situations.

SCALE: 5 = strongly agree
4 = agree
3 = maybe, not certain
2 = disagree
1 = strongly disagree

1. I know what skills I can offer
   employers.   5 4 3 2 1

2. I know what skills employers
   most seek in candidates.   5 4 3 2 1

3. I can clearly explain to employers
   what I do well and enjoy doing.   5 4 3 2 1

4. I can specify why an employer
   should hire me.   5 4 3 2 1

5. I can identify and target employers
   I want to interview.   5 4 3 2 1

6. I can develop a job referral network.   5 4 3 2 1

7. I can prospect for job leads.   5 4 3 2 1

8. I can generate at least one job interview
   for every 10 job search contacts I make.   5 4 3 2 1

9. I can follow-up on job interviews.   5 4 3 2 1

10. I can persuade an employer to
    renegotiate my salary after six
    months on the job.   5 4 3 2 1

11. I know which questions interviewers are most likely to ask me.   5 4 3 2 1

12. If asked to reveal my weaknesses, I know how to respond—answer honestly, but always stress my strengths.   5 4 3 2 1

13. I know how to best dress for the interview.   5 4 3 2 1

14. I know the various types of interviews I may encounter and how to appropriately respond in each situation.   5 4 3 2 1

15. I can easily approach strangers for job information and advice.   5 4 3 2 1

16. I know where to find information on organizations that are most likely to be interested in my skills.   5 4 3 2 1

17. I know how to go beyond vacancy announcements to locate job opportunities appropriate for my qualifications.   5 4 3 2 1

18. I know how to interview appropriate people for job information and advice.   5 4 3 2 1

19. I know many people who can refer me to others for informational interviews.   5 4 3 2 1

20. I can uncover jobs on the hidden job market.   5 4 3 2 1

21. I know how to prepare and practice for the critical job interview.   5 4 3 2 1

22. I know how to stress my positives.   5 4 3 2 1

23. I know how to research the organization and individuals who are likely to interview me.   5 4 3 2 1

24. I have considered how I would respond to illegal questions posed by prospective employers.   5 4 3 2 1

25. I can telephone effectively for job information and employment leads.   5 4 3 2 1

26. I am prepared to conduct an effective telephone interview.   5 4 3 2 1

27. I know when and how to deal with salary questions.   5 4 3 2 1

28. I'm prepared to take a psychological screening test and expect to pass with flying colors.   5 4 3 2 1

29. I know what to read while waiting in the outer office prior to the interview.   5 4 3 2 1

30. I can nonverbally communicate my interest and enthusiasm for the job.   5 4 3 2 1

31. I know the best time to arrive at the interview site.   5 4 3 2 1

32. I know how to respond using positive form and content as well as supports when responding to interviewers' questions.   5 4 3 2 1

33. I know how to summarize my strengths and value at the closing of the interview.   5 4 3 2 1

34. I know what to include in a thank-you letter.   5 4 3 2 1

35. I know when and how to follow-up the interview.   5 4 3 2 1

36. I can explain to interviewers why I made my particular educational choices, including my major and grade point average.   5 4 3 2 1

37. I can clearly explain to interviewers what I like and dislike about particular jobs.   5 4 3 2 1

38. I can clearly explain to interviewers what I want to be doing 5 or 10 years from now.   5 4 3 2 1

39. I have a list of references that can speak in a positive manner about me and my work abilities.   5 4 3 2 1

40. I can clearly state my job and career objectives as both skills and outcomes.   5 4 3 2 1

41. I have set aside 20 hours a week to primarily conduct informational interviews.   5 4 3 2 1

42. I know what foods and drinks are best to select if the interview also includes a luncheon or dinner meeting.   5 4 3 2 1

43. I know how to listen effectively.   5 4 3 2 1

44. I can explain why an employer should hire me.   5 4 3 2 1

45. I know when to use my resume in an informational interview.   5 4 3 2 1

46. I am prepared to handle the salary
question if it comes up early in the
interview.   5 4 3 2 1

47. I can generate three new job leads
each day.   5 4 3 2 1

48. I can outline my major achievements
in my last three jobs and show how
they relate to the job I am interviewing
for.   5 4 3 2 1

49. I know what the interviewer is
looking for when he or she asks
about weaknesses.   5 4 3 2 1

50. I am prepared to handle both series
and stress interviews.   5 4 3 2 1

TOTAL I.Q.   _____

Interpret Your Results

Once you have completed this exercise, add your responses to compute
a total score. This will comprise your composite I.Q. If your score is
between 200 and 250, you seem well prepared to successfully handle the
interview process. If your score is between 150 and 199, you are heading
in the right direction, and this book should help you increase your
interview competencies.

However, if your score falls below 150, you have a great deal of work
to do in preparation for the job interview. This book should quickly help
you achieve a significant increase in your I.Q. The chapters that follow
address each of the above statements either directly or indirectly as they
assist you with the most critical steps in preparing for your informational
and job interviews.

Take Positive Action

If you want to interview for success, you must take certain actions that result in improved interview performance. Like any acquired skill, interviewing requires knowledge, application, and practice. You must take the time and make the effort to seriously follow each step in the interview process. If you put each of the following chapters into practice, you should join the thousands of others who each day experience interview success that results in job offers and jobs that are right for them.

3

Interview Myths & Realities

In Chapter 2 you responded to statements pertaining to your know-ledge, skills, and abilities relevant to the job interview and the goals and desirable actions of the participants. Here, we examine several aspects of the interview again as we discuss key myths and realities affecting the interview situation.

For many applicants job interviewing seems to take place within a big black box. It is shrouded in mystery and apprehension. You don't know what will transpire until you go inside an office to meet an interviewer to discuss the situation. In the meantime, many job hunters can only guess what the interview will be like. They worry about how they should dress, what they should say, when and how to talk about salary, how to close the interview, and if and when it's appropriate to follow-up the interview with a telephone call.

Most aspects of job interviewing are surrounded by myths which contribute to interviewing apprehension. These myths prevent many in-dividuals from properly preparing for the interview.

In this chapter we address 25 of the most common interview myths as well as outline the realities for each. By examining each myth you should be better prepared for the realities of the job interview.

Getting the Job

> **MYTH 1:** My resume will get me the job.
>
> **REALITY:** Your resume helps communicate your qualifications to employers. Resumes are used to screen candidates

and select those to interview. Few people ever get hired on the basis of their resume. Over 95% of employers hire on the basis of a personal interview.

MYTH 2: **The candidate with the best education, skills, and experience will get the job.**

REALITY: Employers hire individuals for many different reasons. Education, skills, and experience are only a few of several hiring criteria. If employers hired only on the basis of education, skills, and experience, they would not need to interview candidates. Such static information is available on applications and resumes. Employers interview because they want to see a warm body—how you look and interact with them, how you would handle various work situations, and how well you will fit into the organization. Other information they can get from other sources. Indeed, the most important reason for hiring you is that the employer "likes" you. How "likes" is defined depends on each employer. In some cases the employer "likes" you because of your educational background, demonstrated skills, and experience. In other cases the employer "likes" you because of your style and personality as well as a gut feeling that you are the right person for the job. The employer will determine or confirm these feelings in the actual job interview. So be prepared in the interview to communicate a great deal of information about yourself other than what the employer already knows—your education, skills, and experience.

Getting the Interview

MYTH 3: **I will get invited to an interview based on the quality of information found in my resume, letters, and applications.**

REALITY: Invitations to interview come from many different sources. Resumes, letters, and applications are important screening devices, but they are by no means the only ones nor the most important. These sources primarily demonstrate qualifications and capabilities in written form. Since most jobs are intensely interpersonal, interviewers also seek verbal and interpersonal sources of information about candidates prior to inviting them to interview. Invitations to interview are initiated from several other job search sources. Networking, referrals, nominations, and the telephone screening interview, for example, are often more important than the more traditional written sources of candidate information. Therefore, it is to your advantage to supplement your written communication with these other sources of information, especially networking for information, advice, and referrals.

MYTH 4: **Once I submit my application for a job, the proper thing to do is to wait until I hear from the employer.**

REALITY: Waiting is not a good job search strategy. It is perfectly acceptable to call the employer within two weeks of submitting your written materials to ask when you might expect to hear about the selection of candidates to be interviewed. Employers often fail to inform candidates whether or not they are still under consideration. It is to your advantage to get a definite "yes" or "no" rather than waste your time doing nothing else in anticipation of being called for an interview.

MYTH 5: **Invitations to interviews normally come by letter or fax.**

REALITY: Most employers issue invitations to interview by telephone. In fact, many interviewers will telephone you in order to conduct a screening interview over the phone. Based on how well you do in this interview, you will be invited by telephone to attend a formal job interview. Therefore, you should be well prepared to handle this telephone screening interview.

Preparing For the Interview

MYTH 6:   **I cannot prepare for interviews because I don't know if I will get an interview nor do I know what the interviewer will ask. It's best to wait and see what happens. Once I'm invited to the interview, I almost have the job.**

REALITY: Everything you have done in your job search thus far—self-assessment, skills identification, objective setting, research, resume and letter writing, networking—has prepared you for the job interview. Based on these activities and the information you have acquired about yourself, the job, and the organization, you can do many additional things to prepare for the interview. Best of all, you can predict and prepare for 80% or more of the questions the interviewer will ask you. And remember, you'll only get the job if you do well in the interview. Preparation will help you do well.

MYTH 7:   **Once I've been invited to the interview, there's not much I can do other than get a good night's sleep so I am fresh for the next day's interview.**

REALITY: There is a great deal you can and should do in preparation for the interview—in addition to getting a good night's sleep. You need to make decisions about your wardrobe; determine how long it will take you to arrive at the interview site and where you will park; review how you will greet the interviewer; examine your files on the organization and collect any additional information about the organization, job, and salary ranges; formulate strategies for and practice the jist of answering questions you expect to be asked, engage in stress reduction techniques; and review what you stated in your resume. It is a good idea to practice interview questions and answers with a friend—you may even wish to tape-record this session. Remember, you must be at your peak performance for this interview—both verbally and non-verbally.

Arriving and Waiting For the Interviewer

MYTH 8: **If I'm late for the interview, it's best to find a good excuse for being late—like bad traffic, no parking places, car problems, illness in family, etc. The interviewer will understand and excuse me.**

REALITY: There is absolutely no excuse, other than personal injury or family tragedy, for being late for the interview. After all, the very first impression you make on the interviewer is your presence. If you arrive late, you make a very bad impression which will negatively affect the rest of the interview. If you can't arrive on time for the interview—regardless of what you consider a legitimate excuse—what will you do when you work for the employer? As part of your preparation, you must review the location of the interview site and determine where you will park. Arrive in the interviewer's building at least 10 to 15 minutes before the scheduled interview time. It's always a good idea to reconfirm the time by calling the interviewer the day before—just in case the interviewer's schedule has changed. Remember, the interview begins when you arrive—not when you meet the interviewer.

MYTH 9: While waiting in the office for the interviewer, I should just sit and wait to be called.

REALITY: Your job interview begins as soon as you walk through the office door. Since you will be under observation, do some positive things that can be observed and reported. For example, if the secretary or receptionist is not too busy, ask some friendly and interested questions about the organization. You may get some important information that will help you in the interview. If the waiting area has some magazines or literature on the organization displayed, pick up and browse through the more organization-relevant and serious literature. Keep in mind the interviewer may ask the secretary or receptionist's opinion about you. If you appeared cold or unfriendly, just sat there like a bump on a log, and appeared disinterested in the organization by reading People Magazine rather than the annual report, these behaviors may be reported to the interviewer.

The Interview

MYTH 10: It's best to show I am an individual by not conforming to standard expectations of how to dress for an interview.

REALITY: Unless you are interviewing for an artistic or creative job, interviewers expect to see conventional attire. However, you need not dress in the traditional navy blue suit interview garb of the 1960s and 1970s. Keep your dress conservative, conventional, and appropriate. Your attire should not distract from your capabilities in the interview.

MYTH 11: I should not wear jewelry or other expensive looking items and clothing to the interview.

REALITY: The best choices of jewelry, accessories, and clothes will vary from one interview situation to another. In general it is okay to wear jewelry and accessories. But do not overdo it with excessive amounts or big and flashy designs. You should wear good quality clothes which need not be expensive.

MYTH 12: **As soon as I enter the interviewer's office, I should sit down, relax, and initiate some small talk about the office, weather, or my trip to the office.**

REALITY: As soon as you enter the office, you should go over to the interviewer, shake hands firmly, stay standing until invited to sit down where the interviewer indicates a seating preference, and wait for the interviewer to initiate a conversation. Maintain good eye contact, do a moderate amount of smiling, and sit with a very slight forward lean toward the interviewer.

MYTH 13: **I should wait for the interviewer to take the initiative in asking questions.**

REALITY: Let the interviewer initiate the first question, but you must also take initiative in asking questions of the interviewer. This is a two way communication situation in which both parties are attempting to exchange useful information. If you take no initiative, you will be seen as someone lacking initiative.

MYTH 14: **The most important time of the interview is during the final five minutes, when I'll be discussing salary, asking about the hiring decision, and closing the interview.**

REALITY: It's how you begin—not how you end—that is most important in the job interview. While the final five minutes are important, the most important time is at the very beginning of the interview—**the first five minutes**. It is during this time you must make an initial impression on the interviewer. During these critical minutes you are greeting the interviewer and getting started with the interview. How you look, smell, and sit will be just as important as what you say. This initial impression will set the tone for the remainder of the interview during which time the interviewer will be reconfirming what he or she already knows and feels about you from the first five minutes.

MYTH 15: **If the interviewer asks if I have any negatives or weaknesses, I should indicate I have none.**

REALITY: You should be honest—but don't be stupid. Everyone has negatives. If you indicate you have none, the interviewer knows you are being less than candid. But neither should you blurt out your worst negatives. Be tactful by turning this possible negative situation into a positive. Talk about a negative that can also be seen as a positive. For example, if asked *"Do you have any weaknesses?"*, you might talk about a weakness that is also a job strength: *"Yes, I often work too late and thus neglect my family. I'm trying to better balance my work and home life."*

MYTH 16: **If I'm asked an illegal question, I should let the interviewer know it's illegal and that he or she should not be asking me such a question.**

REALITY: Yes, you can be perfectly up-front and let the interviewer know you have the law on your side. In fact, you could go so far as to threaten to sue the interviewer for such stupidity. However, this action is not likely to win the job. You might want to handle such a situation with a little tact and humor. For example, if you are asked about your age—an illegal question—point out that *"Since that question is no* *longer supposed to arise in interviews, do you still want me to answer it? I'm a little reluctant to answer it since it could present some future problems for you. I do want to give you all the information you need for determining my qualifications for this position. Let me answer it this way so we will be okay. I won't be ready to retire for another 25 years; I've had my driver's license for more than 10 years; and I'm feeling like I'm not a day over 21. I hope my age won't disqualify me for this position."* At the same time, the interviewer may be well aware this is an illegal question and thus he or she wants to see how well you will handle a potentially stressful situation.

MYTH 17: **I'll be at a disadvantage because the interviewer will feel confident and I'll be nervous.**

REALITY: If you practice some stress reduction techniques, such as taking deep breaths and focusing attention on the questions, you should be able to get through the interview with more confidence. In addition, many interviewers are as nervous as the interviewees— they are under pressure to get accurate information and make the right decision.

MYTH 18: **I should keep my answers as short as possible so the interviewer will have time to ask me more questions.**

REALITY: You should try to answer the questions as thoroughly as possible. Remember, the interviewer is looking for thoughtful answers that indicate some depth on your part. Don't get carried away with lengthy answers but do go from general responses to specifics that indicate your depth.

MYTH 19: **I should avoid talking about anything that would raise questions about my qualifications or abilities to do the job.**

REALITY: You should anticipate possible objections the employer would have to hiring you—your age, sex, experience, employment record, grade point average, etc. Since questioning in many of these areas is illegal for employers, you may wish to address them head-on by raising what you believe would be negative concerns on the part of the employer. But be sure to treat these objections as potential positives rather than negatives. For example, you might say *"I know you might think being female and married will present problems for this job. However, my family is very supportive of my career. I enjoy this kind of work. I am willing to travel, and my family life has never interfered with my getting the job done. In fact, my stable family life has been a real asset on the job. I stay with my employers and am a very responsible person."*

You address in a positive manner concerns you believe the prospective employer will have about some aspect of your background or present situation, but that she may not be able to ask about because of legal prohibitions. If you say nothing, the concern remains and may take you out of the running.

MYTH 20: **My major goal in the interview is to get the job.**

REALITY: Your major goal should be the same as the interviewer's—gain useful information from which you can make a decision about joining this organization. If you make this your goal, the interview will become more like a friendly two-way dialogue rather than a stressful inquisition. Both you and the interviewer will go away with the information the two of you need to make good decisions.

Negotiating Salaries and Benefits

MYTH 21: **I should state my salary requirements on my resume or early in the interview.**

REALITY: You should **never** state your salary requirements on your resume. Defer this issue until the very end of the employment interview—after you have received a job offer and you have entered into the salary negotiation stage. Up until that point everything you have done in relation to this position should be aimed at communicating your **value** to the employer. It is difficult to talk about salary when you have yet to determine the duties of the position or demonstrate your value. Only after you have completed the interview are you ready to talk about money. If the interviewer tries to bring up the money question early in the interview, try to delay your answer until the end of the interview. For example, you might say, *"If you don't mind, I would rather address the salary question after I've had a chance to learn more about this position."*

MYTH 22: **To get the job, I should settle for a lower salary than I and the job are worth. I can negotiate better terms at my first performance review.**

REALITY: You should go after the highest possible figure both you and job are worth. Employers are willing to pay for good performance. If you have to settle for less than what both you and the job are worth, seriously consider looking for another job. You will probably be unhappy knowing you are underpaid. And the performance review may not be translated into a higher salary. Your initial base salary will largely determine your future salary increases.

MYTH 23: **Once I'm offered the job, I should immediately let the employer know whether or not I'll accept it.**

REALITY: Don't rush into such a decision. While it is flattering to receive an offer, take your time to decide whether this job is right for you. It is perfectly acceptable to ask to consider the offer over a 48-hour period. For positions that require relocation or for executive positions, a week or longer to consider an offer is not unusual. During that time you should assess the offer in relation to your career goals as well as any alternative jobs you are considering. If, for example, you are considering another job, inform the other employer that you have a job offer and would appreciate knowing where you stand since you must make a decision. Such an approach may hasten another hiring decision and thus provide you two offers to compare as well as negotiate employment terms.

Close and Follow-Up

MYTH 24: **The interviewer is the one who closes the interview and lets me know if and when he or she will contact me.**

REALITY: You must also take the initiative during the closing of the interview. One of the of best approaches is to summarize your understanding of the job and your strengths. In addition, ask the interviewer when he or she expects to make the hiring decision or schedule the next round of interviews. This closing question will let you know how long you should expect to wait before hearing from the employer. It is perfectly acceptable to follow the hiring decision question with this question: *"If I have not heard from you by Friday (or whatever is appropriate given the employer's time line), may I give you a call?"* Assuming the answer is *"yes"* and you indeed follow-up, you will either eliminate or include this employer for future consideration. And this is exactly what you want to do. The sooner you can eliminate employers from consideration, the sooner you can mentally move on to other potential employers.

MYTH 25: Once I've completed the interview, all I can do is wait for the employer to contact me as to whether I have been selected for the position.

REALITY: Again, waiting is not a positive job search strategy. You must take initiative at this point. Within 24 hours you should send a thank you letter to the interviewer emphasizing: (1) the professional manner in which the interview took place, (2) your continuing interest in the company and position, and (3) how your qualifications fit the employer's needs. Since few interviewers receive thank you letters following an interview, your letter should stand out. This can become one of the most powerful approaches to getting the job.

If you overcome these myths by following our realities, you will be well prepared to interview for success. You will impress upon employers that you should be offered the job.

4

Organize Your Job Search

C onducted within a larger job search context, interviews are only one of several important job search activities. Including self-assessment, skills identification, objective setting, research, resume and letter production, and networking, these other activities are related to one another and take place in **sequence** to each other. All lead to the job interview. Interviews normally occur only **after** completing all of the other activities. Understanding how these activities relate to one another is important for conducting the job interview as well as for putting the remainder of these chapters into practice.

If you've not done so yet, you undoubtedly will engage in several job search activities sometime prior to the interview. The important question is how well you will conduct each of these activities and thus the critical job interview. In this chapter we present a brief overview of the key job search activities and examine how they relate to your job interview.

Get Started With Useful Resources

Each year millions of job hunters turn to career planning books for assistance. Normally they begin with a general book and next turn to a resume and letter writing book. An interview book—if they can find one—is often a third choice.

The reasons for choosing this sequence of books is simple. Job hunters should begin with a sound understanding of all elements contributing to a successful job search and then focus on specific activities which have the greatest payoffs: resumes, letters, and interviews.

If this book represents your first career planning book, you may want to supplement it with other books listed in our resource section. Many of these books are available in your local library and bookstore or can be ordered directly from Impact Publications by completing the order form at the end of this book. Impact Publications also publishes a brochure of additional job and career resources. To receive a free copy of this listing, send a self-addressed, stamped envelope (#10 business size) to:

IMPACT PUBLICATIONS
ATTN: Free Careers Brochure
9104-N Manassas Drive
Manassas Park, VA 20111-5211

You also may want to visit their World Wide Web site for a complete listing of career resources: *http://www.impactpublications.com.* Their site contains some of the most important career and job finding resources available today, including many titles that are difficult, if not impossible, to find in bookstores and libraries. You will find everything from additional resume books, to books on self-assessment, cover letters, interviewing, government and international jobs, military, women, minorities, students, and entrepreneurs. The catalog also includes videos, audio programs, computer software, subscriptions, and CD-ROM programs relating to jobs and careers. This is an excellent resource for keeping in touch with the major resources that can assist you with every stage of your job search.

> **Try this World Wide Web site for the latest information on resources for conducting a dynamite job search:**
> *http://www.impactpublications.com*

Do It Right

It is important to understand how to best get a job by focusing on methods and strategies appropriate for conducting an effective job search. Unfortunately, few books place the interview within the larger context of the job search. Similarly, many people emphasize only one or two job search activities. They fail to understand they must become proficient in several different, yet related, job search activities simultaneously.

Take, for example, resumes. Many resume books crowd bookstore shelves with example after example of supposedly outstanding resumes. Most of these books are long on form but short on content. They encourage you to edit a favorite example and use it as your own—a form of creative plagiarism. Such books are misleading. They fail to warn the reader that effective resumes are the product of four other related job search activities: self-assessment, skills identification, objective setting, and research. Failure to engage in these activities **prior to** writing the resume will most likely result in producing attractive but ineffective resumes. In other words, you may get the **form** right but you will lack important **content**.

Many interview books tend to be written from a similar narrow, copy-cat perspective. Concentrating solely on the job interview in isolation of the other critical job search steps, many interview books are misleading. Emphasizing form, they assume somehow content will follow. They give readers a false sense of self-confidence by teaching them to **play a role** devoid of much substantive content. Readers, for example, are rehearsed on anticipated questions/answers and expected interview behaviors. They are presented with example after example of typical interview questions and canned responses.

Anticipating questions is fine, but devising canned answers designed to impress the interviewer rather than communicate accurate information about the candidate borders on unethical job search practices. The basis for truthfully answering such interview questions is found in the self-assessment and skills identification steps of the job search—steps which should have been completed long before writing a resume or accepting an invitation to interview for a position.

Our approach to interviewing assumes a certain degree of **preparation** on your part **before** entering the interview stage. You should have already completed the self-assessment, skills identification, objective setting, research, resume production, and networking stages. If you have completed these steps, you should be well prepared to address interviewers' questions with substantive answers about your skills, capabilities, achievements, and goals-important areas of questioning for interviewers. If you have not done so already, we encourage you to understand the larger picture—the critical career development and job search processes which are related to the job interview. You must acquire the substantive content necessary for playing the interviewee role.

Understand the Career Development Process

What are the career development and job search processes you need to understand and implement? How do they relate to the job interview? These questions are partly answered in the figure on page 35.

The career development process consists of four sets of development activities. As illustrated on page 35, the interview occupies an important position in the skill development and implementation stages (Panels 3 and 4). Prior to developing interview skills and actually conducting a job interview, you should assess your strengths (Panel 1) as well as explore career information (Panel 2) relating to jobs, careers, organizations, individuals, and communities. Only then will you be prepared to thoroughly develop and focus specific job search activities (Panel 3) and conduct a job search (Panel 4) which focuses on jobs and careers that are right for you.

Specific Job Search Steps

The Figure on page 36 further elaborates the job search process. It relates the career development skills within a comprehensive job search campaign. The seven distinct job search steps are related sequentially.

Underlying this job search model is an important assumption about how people should best seek employment. In short, they should go after high quality employment by looking for jobs and careers that directly relate to their **strengths**. These strengths consist of interests, motivations, skills, and accomplishments (page 35, Panel 1). Accordingly, they should seek jobs that they **do well and enjoy doing**.

Failing to use this positive approach, most people look for advertised job openings and then try to fit their qualifications into the job. In other words, they try to **fit into jobs rather than find jobs that are fit for them**. Such a strategy does lead to finding jobs, but it often leads to low quality jobs and unhappy employees and employers; it stresses one's weaknesses rather than one's strengths. We assume, on the other hand, you want to prepare for employment that is compatible with your particular mix of strengths and motivations—a job that is fit for you!

THE CAREER DEVELOPMENT PROCESS

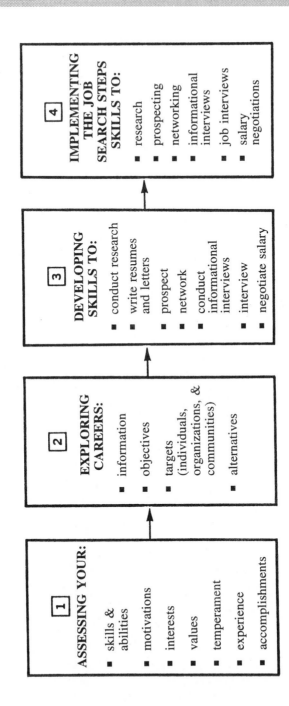

1 ASSESSING YOUR:

- skills & abilities
- motivations
- interests
- values
- temperament
- experience
- accomplishments

2 EXPLORING CAREERS:

- information
- objectives
- targets (individuals, organizations, & communities)
- alternatives

3 DEVELOPING SKILLS TO:

- conduct research
- write resumes and letters
- prospect
- network
- conduct informational interviews
- interview
- negotiate salary

4 IMPLEMENTING THE JOB SEARCH STEPS SKILLS TO:

- research
- prospecting
- networking
- informational interviews
- job interviews
- salary negotiations

JOB SEARCH STEPS

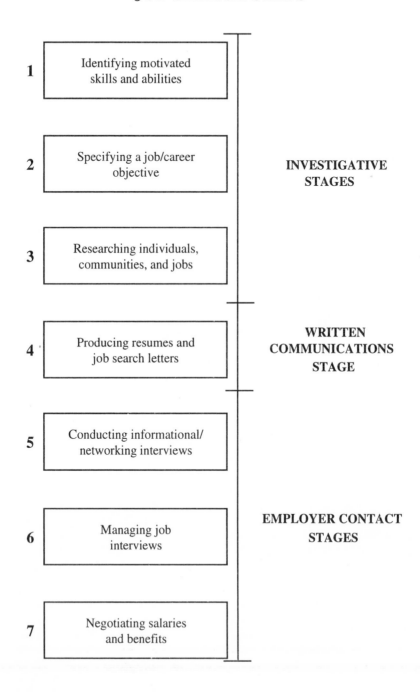

Identify Your Strengths

If you opt for our high quality employment strategy, you should follow the career development and job search steps outlined in pages 35 and 36. Begin by identifying your motivated skills and abilities. Find out exactly what you do well (skills, abilities, accomplishments) and enjoy doing (values, motivations). In other words, you want to identify your **motivated abilities**. These motivated abili-ties also become your **strengths**.

And it is your strengths you must communicate to potential employers. At the very least, you need to know your strengths and communicate them in a language appropriate to a job search.

You will find several self-directed and counselor-assisted assessment techniques available to help you generate information on your motivated abilities and strengths.

> **Find out what you do well and enjoy doing—these become your motivated skills and abilities.**

The following exercise (page 38), for example, should quickly result in identifying your key achievements. This information should play a central role in communicating your strengths to employers on your resume and during the job interview.

After completing these exercises, put them in a file so you can quickly refer to the information as you prepare for the job interview. The interviewer **will** want to know about your achievements and work values. The more details you can supply during the interview, the stronger will be your interview performance. The information you generate in these exercises provides you with concrete examples from which you can communicate your strengths and values.

For more information on these and other self-directed exercises to help you uncover important information on yourself, consult some of the books listed in the resource section at the end of this book. Many of these books outline different techniques for identifying your job and career strengths.

KEY ACHIEVEMENTS

INSTRUCTIONS: Prioritize what you believe are your most important achievements in your life. An achievement is anything you enjoyed doing, felt you did well, and developed a sense of satisfaction, accomplishment, and pride in doing. Make five copies of this form and complete one form for each accomplishment.

ACHIEVEMENT #__: _____

_____

1. **How did I get involved?** _____

    _____

    _____

2. **What did I do?** _____

    _____

    _____

    _____

3. **How did I do it?** _____

    _____

    _____

4. **What did I especially enjoy about doing it?** _____

    _____

    _____

    _____

    _____

The following exercises focus on identifying your work values. It is important to know these **before** you accept a job.

10 THINGS I LIKE
MOST ABOUT MY WORK

INSTRUCTIONS: List the 10 things you most like about your present and past jobs. Identify them in the order of preference.

1. _____
2. _____
3. _____
4. _____
5. _____
6. _____
7. _____
8. _____
9. _____
10. _____

10 THINGS I MOST
DISLIKE ABOUT MY WORK

INSTRUCTIONS: List what you feel are 10 of your major job frustrations and dissatisfactions. Start with the things you most dislike.

1. _____
2. _____
3. _____
4. _____
5. _____

6. _____

7. _____

8. _____

9. _____

10. _____

Job and Career Objectives

Knowing what you **really want to do** is the second critical job search step. If you lack a job or career objective, you will have extreme difficulty writing a coherent resume as well as communicating your purpose in job interviews. Therefore, it is essential that you complete this step.

Your job objective should be centered on your strengths as well as on employers' needs; it links your key skills to expected outcomes for employers. In other words, it should state what you plan to accomplish for employers given your primary skills. Try stating your job objective by completing this simple exercise:

MY JOB OBJECTIVE

I prefer a job that will use by ability to <u>develop new markets</u>
(your primary skill)

that will result in <u>increased profits and market shares</u>.
(expected outcomes for the employer)

Being a **work-centered objective**, it communicates that you are a skilled, purposeful, and productive individual. Employers want to hire such people. Again, several of the books listed in the resource section outline how to develop a strong job and career objective.

Writing Resumes and Doing Research

Your resume is your calling card for opening the doors of employers. It advertises you for interviews. Therefore, everything in your resume should relate to your strengths and objective. Prior to writing your resume, you should conduct research (Step 4) on different jobs, careers, individuals, organizations, and communities which relate to your strengths and interests. This research will help you better target your resume and job search letters.

While much research can be conducted in libraries, the best research comes from talking to knowledgeable people, especially those in hiring positions. These people will give you valuable information and advice on the job market, your job search, and potential employers. In Chapters 6 and 7 we outline how to do much of this research.

Conducting Preliminary Interviews

When you conduct research by interviewing people, you will acquire important information and develop key job search contacts for future reference. These contacts will help you locate job opportunities which are not advertised. This type of research, in effect, becomes what we call the informational/networking interview.

Occurring prior to formal job interviews, informational/networking interviews are the most effective way to open the doors of potential employers. If you neglect to conduct these interviews, your job search will be more difficult. You will be forced to rely on employment listings for job leads. If you spend most of your time responding to such listings, your odds of getting a job interview will be lower than if you diversify your approach. On the other hand, informational/networking interviews put you in the right places at the right time to learn about potential job openings **before** they are ever publicized.

Because of the importance of informational/networking interviews in relation to formal job interviews, we devote a separate chapter to this subject (Chapter 6).

Interviewing For Jobs and Money

We divide the job interview into two steps. The formal job interview (Step 6) is the major focus of this book. Salary negotiation (Step 7, Chapter 11) is one part of the interview. It normally occurs near the end of the employment interview—immediately before or after the job offer, depending on how the employer decides to close the interview. These two steps are extremely important when you consider the following rules for job search success: no interview, no job offer; no job offer, no salary negotiations; and no salary negotiations without a job interview.

If you wish further information on each of the job search steps, examine some of the books included in the resource section. We especially recommend *High Impact Resumes and Letters*, *Change Your Job Change Your Life*, *Dynamite Networking For Dynamite Jobs*, and *Discover the Best Jobs For You*. All of these comprehensive books use the same career development and job search framework developed in this book. For a greater in-depth treatment of salary negotiations, see our *Dynamite Salary Negotiations: Know What You're Worth, and Get It!*

Investing Time and Effort

Preparing for interviews and conducting other job search activities takes time and effort. A successful job search, consisting of 15 to 25 hours of job search activities each week, will normally take three months to complete. Some people complete their job search within a few days whereas others may take up to six months. But remember, we are dealing with a particular type of individual. They seek jobs that directly relate to their strengths and motivations rather than any job that looks interesting and available. These are selective and highly successful people who set goals, plan, and persist in achieving their goals. Like most people, they experience disappointments, rejections, and frustrations. But unlike many other people, they learn how to handle rejections and view them as learning experiences. They realize acceptances only come after encountering and overcoming many rejections. More specifically, these people possess three critical characteristics associated with successful entrepreneurs: drive, persistence and a positive attitude.

> **Successful people are prepared to communicate their value to employers.**

The following chapters represent the nuts-and-bolts of interviewing. They are designed to help you join the increasing number of successful and satisfied job hunters who effectively manage their job search. These successful people are especially adept at managing the critical job interview. When they receive an invitation to interview, they are prepared to communicate their **value** to employers. Employers **hire** them because they **like** them and believe they will add value to the organization.

You, too, can join this group if you both understand and **practice** the advice outlined in the next nine chapters. In the end, the time and effort spent in preparation for the job interview will be well worth it when the employer finally turns to you and says *"You're hired!"*

5

Encounter Different Interviews

Interviewers use several different types of interviews, questions, and techniques to determine your capabilities. Therefore, it is to your advantage to be well prepared for a variety of possible interview situations, questions, and techniques as well as different types of interviews. It is always better to be prepared for both expected and unexpected interviews and interviewers than to blow the interview because you were caught off guard with a surprise interview.

You may, for example, interview several times with a single employer or have a single interview with several individuals. Some interviewers are seasoned professionals who know how to conduct good interviews. Others may be amateurs who know little about how to elicit or convey the information both you and the organization need to make the best decision.

Before examining how to prepare for a successful interview, let's look at various types of employment interviews. You should be aware of these since you may unexpectedly encounter one of the less frequent interview types sometime during the interview process. If you are asked to return for a second or third interview with the same organization, you may face a different type of interview than during the first round of interviews.

This brings up an important point. Thus far we have referred to **a** successful job interview. For many positions—especially professional or management level positions—you will face more than one interview. In some cases you will go through three or four interviews. Each interview may consist of interviews with several individuals.

Interview Types

You may encounter several types of interviews throughout the course of your job search. On page 46, we outline a framework for understanding and relating different interview goals, types, settings, and techniques. While you may not experience all of these interviews, you may encounter several of them.

Central to our interview typology is a concern with the objectives or goals of interviewers. While your ultimate goal is to get the right job, you may also have other goals. From the interviewee's perspective, other objectives may include gathering information about the job opening; acquiring advice about your job search if the present opening doesn't seem to be a good fit with your skills, abilities, and knowledge; receiving referrals for job openings that may be more appropriate within this firm or with other firms; or getting invitations to additional interviews. In the end, pursuing these goals may be more important to your job search than getting a job offer for the opening you came hoping to fill.

Informational/Networking Interviews

Often overlooked by job seekers, informational/networking interviews are an important step toward the ultimate goal of landing the job. Once you have an objective and identify what you do well and enjoy doing, you should talk with people working in your area of interest. Such interviews will give you valuable information about particular jobs and careers, especially the skills and experience employers expect you to have for different jobs. This type of interview also yields important job information and helps develop referral networks. The networks consist of individuals who serve as job contacts in your field of interest. Best of all, these interviews often lead directly to formal job interviews.

> **Informational/networking interviews often lead directly to formal job interviews.**

Informational/networking interviews can be one of the most powerful job search strategies you employ. In order to make them work for you, follow this guiding principle: **never ask for a job; always ask for information, advice, and referrals.** As a result, you will acquire useful

INTERVIEW SITUATION: TYPES, SETTINGS, QUESTIONING TECHNIQUES AND STRUCTURE

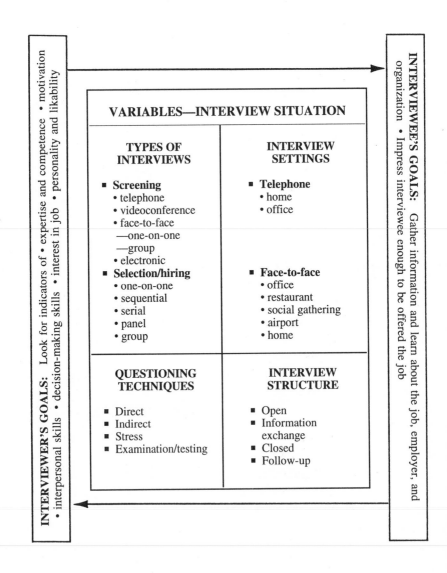

INTERVIEWER'S GOALS: Look for indicators of • expertise and competence • motivation • interpersonal skills • decision-making skills • interest in job • personality and likability

INTERVIEWEE'S GOALS: Gather information and learn about the job, employer, and organization • Impress interviewee enough to be offered the job

VARIABLES—INTERVIEW SITUATION

TYPES OF INTERVIEWS

- **Screening**
  - telephone
  - videoconference
  - face-to-face
    —one-on-one
    —group
  - electronic
- **Selection/hiring**
  - one-on-one
  - sequential
  - serial
  - panel
  - group

INTERVIEW SETTINGS

- **Telephone**
  - home
  - office
- **Face-to-face**
  - office
  - restaurant
  - social gathering
  - airport
  - home

QUESTIONING TECHNIQUES

- Direct
- Indirect
- Stress
- Examination/testing

INTERVIEW STRUCTURE

- Open
- Information exchange
- Closed
- Follow-up

information as well as receive invitations to interview which may result in job offers.

Your informational/networking interviews should be conducted with friends, relatives, acquaintances, and strangers. While most of these people do not have job openings in your area of interest, they do have important resources—information, advice, and networks—relevant to your job search. You request these interviews in order to gain access to their resources. Your goal is **not** to get a job with these people—only useful information, advice, and contacts for more information, advice and referrals. In addition, you want to be **remembered** so that these people will keep you in mind for future job openings and additional referrals. Chapter 6 examines the informational/networking interview in greater detail.

Screening Interviews

Employment interviews are normally conducted when there are actual or anticipated job openings. The first such interview is often a **screening interview**. The employer's goal is as the term implies—screen people in or out of further consideration. For example, an employer may have a pool of ten promising applicants. Wishing to narrow the number for face-to-face interviews, the employer calls each candidate to inquire about their employment status, gather more information on their qualifications and identify cues regarding their appropriateness for the position. These telephone interviews will result in eliminating most of the applicants.

Employers conduct telephone screening interviews with greater frequency these days—especially when many of their applicants are from out of town. Even when the applicants and the employer are located in the same community, the employer may choose to screen applicants first by telephone. Such interviews are more efficient and cost effective in eliminating a large number of applicants than face-to-face interviews. While the telephone interview may take only five minutes, an office interview may take an hour or more. As interviewing costs increase, we can expect the use of screening interviews to increase accordingly.

If you receive a phone call from an employer, assume you are being screened for an interview. Take this interview as seriously as you would any interview. What you say and how you say it may determine whether you will be invited to a selection/hiring interview.

With this in mind, it is advisable to have an area by your phone equipped with everything you need to handle a telephone screening call with aplomb. A pencil and notepad, a calendar (up to date with commitments noted) as well as a copy of your resume are the minimal items. It is also a good idea to have a list of the organizations and names of individuals to whom you have sent your resume as well as any job descriptions if you have responded to advertised vacancies. It is not a bad idea to carry a copy of these items in your briefcase as well—in a folder away from prying eyes at the office.

If you receive a screening phone call at a bad time—you are at the office and can't talk freely or you are at home with a pot on the range that is about to boil over. Rather than take the call and come across ineptly, ask if you can call the employer back in ten minutes—or whatever fits the situation. Make certain you have the company name and the correct name and phone number of the person you are to call. If at work, go to an office where you can close the door and talk with some privacy. If at home, get the problem situation under control then place the call to the employer. In either situation, take a few minutes to prepare mentally for the call. Check over any notes you have on the organization, glance over your resume, take a deep breath, and dial.

You want to come across as professional, yet dynamic, on the telephone. It is harder to be as animated on the phone as you may be in face-to-face communication, but it is important that you convey both warmth and enthusiasm. When there are no visual cues available to the interviewer, your vocal cues take on greater importance. Engage in positive non-verbal behaviors: smile when a smile is appropriate to the verbal message. Sit up erect at a desk or table (you will be and will sound more alert). Avoid being dressed too casually—get out of that bathrobe. If you are dressed for business, both your language and paralanguage will convey greater professionalism.

Positive verbal behaviors for the telephone interview include:

- project your voice
- enunciate clearly
- use complete sentences except for occasional "yes" or "no" responses
- use good grammar
- avoid pauses—vocalized or not (silent pauses in many situations are a plus, but on the phone they lose their use as emphasis or as an indication of a thoughtful response and come across as dead space)

- speak at a comfortable pace—don't rush, but don't be overly slow
- modulate your voice toward its lowest natural range

Practice with a tape recorder and you'll get a good idea how others hear you on the telephone. Make modifications, if necessary, and record yourself again. Keep working on this until you are satisfied with how you project yourself on the telephone. Clear, professional, and dynamic communication should be your goal.

Screening interviews also take place in face-to-face settings, such as college placement offices, employment firms, and job fairs. The job of the screener is to weed out and reject all but the best qualified candidates. The person conducting the screening interview is likely to be from the human resources department of the company that has the opening or a representative from an employment firm retained by the company. Your goal here is to be selected in the group to be passed on for selection/ hiring interviews. While you don't have to prove you are the best quali-fied at this point, you do have to impress the interviewer that you are

> ## The employer's goal is to screen people in or out of further consideration.

qualified. Recruiters from public and private organizations regularly visit college campuses across the country to interview graduating seniors. In most instances they will screen candidates—determine which ones to invite for further interviews.

Employment firms, both public and private, function as gatekeepers in screening applicants for employers. They meet with applicants to determine whether to refer them to particular employers for job inter-views. Designed mainly to benefit employers, this screening process saves them a great deal of recruitment time—and money.

Job fairs are sponsored by employers who wish to meet many job applicants to exchange information and conduct preliminary screening interviews. Normally applicants at job fairs listen to presentations by employers and circulate their resumes to interested companies. The employers meet with the prospective applicants in order to identify which ones to invite to a job interview at a later date. This whole process of circulating resumes and meetings between employers and candidates is one of screening for information prior to a formal job interview.

Videoconferencing

Videoconferencing interviews are used for many of the same reasons as the telephone screening interview. They save time and money. They allow the employer to get impressions of the candidate without the expense of flying a candidate in for an interview. Since videoconferencing allows the interviewer to see as well as hear the candidate, it provides more information than a telephone interview.

Nearly half the largest U.S. corporations use videoconferencing to communicate with their offices in various geographical locations. So it is natural that they see the value of applying this technology to the interview selection process—using it primarily as a screening tool for mid-management and executive candidates. A number of firms now offer facilities for videoconferencing and rent studio time. In the Washington, D.C. Metro area, for example, Kinkos and Sprint have teamed to offer videoconferencing at their business centers. They provide the studio and charge $150.00 for a 30-minute session.

A version of interactive videoconferencing called InterView is now available at many universities. This technology provides a more convenient and less expensive way for employers to screen college seniors than sending recruiters to campuses to hold screening interviews.

Read back over the positive verbal behaviors for the telephone screening interview on pages 48-49—they all apply to videoconferencing as well. In addition, pay attention to the way you are attired, your facial expression and your posture. See Chapter 8 for tips on appropriate attire for the interview. Remember, this **is** an interview. If you are not selected "in" at this point, you will not get the chance for a selection/hiring interview. The camera adds to the situational constraints. Avoid bright colors or prints that could look busy or "dance" on camera. Keep your facial expression enthusiastic, but professional. Sit up straight (no hunched shoulders) with a slight forward lean and keep your hands away from your face and hair.

If you have a chance to videotape yourself at home prior to your interview, watch for mannerisms that focus attention on themselves and hence distract the interviewer from your message. Common distracting mannerisms include:

- rocking back and forth
- fiddling with jewelry

- clenching or massaging your hands
- fixing or brushing back your hair
- crossing your arms—viewed as an exclusion and defensive behavior

As for any interview, be prepared, breathe deeply, concentrate on your message, and channel nervous energy into a dynamic delivery.

Electronic Screening Interviews

A new method for screening job applicants is the use of computerized questions to elicit information before the applicant meets the hiring official. The applicant is initially asked to sit at a computer terminal and respond to a series of questions that will also be "scored" electronically. Though used at present primarily by larger firms, the method may "catch on." If you face this situation, you should do better if you have some understanding of what is taking place.

Employers who use this method believe electronic screening has several advantages. First, the computer presentation poses exactly the same questions in the same way to all applicants and will "score" the responses thus supposedly taking some of the subjectivity out of this portion of the interview.

Second, many hiring officials and placement officers suggest that individuals seem to be more "comfortable" answering questions in the privacy of the one-on-one session with the computer terminal and hence respond more honestly. Some people, it seems, will admit to any-thing—even to stealing from a previous employer—in the computer questioning situation.

Third, the computer can "score" your responses quickly. Several questions are designed with purposeful redundancy in order to identify the individual who is not responding honestly but trying to skew the results a certain way. The computerized scoring will identify the inconsistencies and this information will be available to the human interviewer who conducts the subsequent face-to-face interview. In some instances the scoring programs are designed so that inconsistencies in response rates as well as responses are noted. In other words, if you take a significantly longer time to answer certain questions than is **your** norm for the majority of questions, the questions you pondered excessively will be noted.

The interviewer whom you meet with following your session at the computer terminal will no doubt probe areas in which your responses or response rate seemed to indicate inconsistencies or longer than usual hesitations. The interviewer will assume that you may have problems or something to hide in these areas. If you have read the following sections in this book which help you prepare for interview questions and how to present your responses in an honest, yet positive manner, you should be able to handle the face-to-face follow-up to the electronic screening interview.

Selection/Hiring Interviews

Many people think of the selection/hiring interview as the "real interview." In many respects it is. This interview will be conducted in greater depth than the screening interview. It also will have greater consequences for you and your future.

Most applicants expect only one person to conduct the selection/hiring interview and expect it to take place in an office setting. Although perhaps this is the most common format, these interviews can vary in terms of the number of people involved as well as different settings. There are five basic formats for hiring interviews. They are one-to-one, sequential, serial, panel or a group interview.

One-to-One Interviews

One-to-one, face-to-face interviews are the most common type faced by interviewees. The applicant and the employer meet, usually at the employer's office, and sit down to discuss the position and the applicant's skills, knowledge, and abilities as they relate to the job. At some point, though hopefully late in the interview, salary considerations as well as other benefits may be discussed.

While a screening interview is often conducted by someone in personnel—after all, screening is one of their major functions—hiring decisions are usually made by department managers for lower and many mid-level positions, and by upper management for top-level positions. If the hiring interview is conducted by someone from the department which has the position, you can expect the interviewer to ask many specific job-content questions. If the interviewer is from personnel, the questions will tend to be more general.

Sequential Interviews

For many positions, especially those beyond entry-level, more than one interview will be necessary. Sequential interviews are simply a series of interviews with the decision being made to screen the candidate in or out after each interview. The candidates who are screened in are called back for additional interviews. Although each of the sequential interviews is most frequently a one-to-one interview, you could meet with more than one interviewer at the same time in any of these sessions. You may meet with the same person in each interview, but it is more likely you will meet with new people in subsequent interviews.

When sequential interviews are planned, many of the terms of employment issues such as salary and benefits may not be discussed in the initial interview. These considerations may be saved until later interviews—after the pool of candidates has been narrowed and the employer is getting serious about only a very few candidates. This can work to your advantage since with each interview you should have the opportunity to find out more about the position—ask in subsequent interviews some things you wish you had asked, but forgot, in your initial interview—as well as continue to demonstrate your value to the employer.

Serial Interviews

Serial interviews also consist of several interviews, one after the other. However, with serial interviews the series has been set up from the time the interview was scheduled and no decision will be made until all the interviews have been completed. Usually each meeting is with a different person or group of people, and all the interviews will be held over a one or two day period. Following these interviews, the individuals you met will get together to compare notes and make a collective hiring decision.

> During serial interviews, treat each successive interview as if it were your first.

Many candidates for university faculty positions, for example, encounter a series of interviews that span two days or more. Having flown or driven into town the night before, the next morning a member of the department will pick them up at their hotel. The morning may consist of three meetings: a breakfast meeting, a meeting with the department chairperson, and a meeting with one or two other faculty members as time and class schedules permit (SERIAL INTERVIEWS). The candidate will go to lunch with three or four of the faculty (PANEL INTERVIEW) and in the afternoon meet with the Dean of the Faculty and later successively with two or three other faculty members (SERIAL INTERVIEWS). During the evening a dinner meeting may be scheduled at the department chair's or a faculty member's home (PANEL-SERIAL INTERVIEWS). The next day consists of meeting with any faculty not seen individually on day one (SERIAL) and perhaps being asked to teach a segment of a class (TEST—more on this in Chapter 7).

The most important thing to remember during series interviews is to treat each successive interview as if it were your first. Indeed, for the person interviewing you, it is **their** first interview with you. Although it may be difficult to spread your interests, enthusiasm, and attention equally among the interviewers, it is important to do so. Try to listen just as attentively and answer as fully and carefully with each interviewer as you did with the first interviewer. As your time with one interviewer draws to a close, try to get information on the next person you will meet with. Especially if you have "hit it off" with your present interviewer, you may gain valuable insights into areas of concern that may exist for the next interviewer you will meet.

Panel Interviews

Panel interviews occur infrequently, but they do happen and thus you should know how to best handle them. In a panel interview you are interviewed by several people at the same time. Many Foreign Service Officers remember this as one of the dreaded experiences they encountered when being hired by the State Department. Panel interviews often take place in a pressure-cooker atmosphere. Even when not intended to be stressful, panel interviews are more stressful than other types of interviews. You are subjected to numerous and sometime hostile questions simultaneously. For example,

Panel Questions

"Why did you take only one year of French rather than three?"

"Your grades suggest you're not a peak performer. Why didn't you do better?"

"I find that hard to believe. Why wouldn't you work harder at overcoming that problem?"

"How are you going to increase sales if you've never worked in a marketing department or made major sales presentations? I'm having problems with your lack of experience in this area."

Worst of all, you will have extreme difficulty controlling this interview because you are in an inherently reactive situation. As you answer one person's question, it is hard to gauge how other panel members are responding. Or what will you do if there is an obvious difference of opinion between two panel members and one asks you a pointed question? You may gain the support of one, but lose the support of the other.

Group Interviews

While not common, group interviews do take place. If you find yourself being interviewed along with several other applicants, you are in a group interview. No, the employer is not trying to save money by interviewing several job candidates at once. The employer is using the group setting to glean information not thought to be readily accessible in a one-on-one interview.

> In group interviews the employer will observe applicants' interpersonal skills.

In group interviews the employer will observe the interpersonal skills of applicants. How well a candidate interacts with peers—other applicants—is thought to be an indicator of how well that individual will get along with co-workers. Often a question will be posed to the group or the group will be given a problem to solve. If an applicant exhibits positive leadership behaviors in the group setting, employers tend to believe that person can take charge and be a leader in the workplace. The employer will be looking for positive skills—the ability of an interviewee to draw other candidates into the discussion, to ask questions, to act as peace maker if necessary, to summarize salient points, and to keep the group focused on the task at hand and moving toward the goal.

We know of an applicant for a teaching position in a graduate level program that enrolls older adults. The school prides itself on its non-traditional program and the fact that its faculty are not lecturers, but facilitators of the learning process. Our friend, who was used to interviewing in more traditional university settings, was at first chagrined to find herself in what she now knows was a group interview. Somewhat into the two hour session she caught on. The "observers" were only mildly interested in the content of the group's discussion. The real news was the interpersonal communication that was unfolding. Once she realized the focus of the inquiry, she modified her behaviors and did quite well. It would seem though that some candidates never did see the light as they argued tooth and nail to win their particular point of view.

Questioning Techniques

Direct

You will most likely encounter the direct question approach. Interviewers tend to use this method because it allows them to control the direction of the interview. By posing specific questions to each interviewee, interviewers find it much easier to compare one candidate with another.

The interviewer who uses the direct questioning technique has specific questions and usually asks these in a planned sequence. Usually the interviewer is interested in finding out about your:

- Education
- Work Experience
- Career Goals
- Personality
- Skills and Strengths
- Ability to take initiative and solve problems
- Demonstrated ability to handle particular situations

The direct questioning technique involves both open-ended and closed questions. Closed questions are those that can be answered with a simple "yes" or "no." Although candidates often will elaborate beyond the simple "yes" or "no," even these elaborations are more concise and to the point than answers to open-ended questions. Open-ended questions must be answered with more than a "yes" or "no" and often begin with "what" or "how."

Open-Ended and Closed Questions

"Did you complete our application form?" (CLOSED)

"Would you like a cup of coffee?" (CLOSED)

"Did you ever work for _____?" (CLOSED—but you may decide to elaborate on this one)

"How did you like working for _____?" (OPEN-ENDED)

"What do you think about _____?" (OPEN-ENDED)

"How would you handle _____?" (OPEN-ENDED)

Indirect

The indirect interview technique is less structured than the direct method. It is also used less frequently than the direct method. When using this method, the interviewer wants you to talk as much as possible about yourself and the job so he or she can determine your overall performance in this interview. The interviewer tends to ask broad general questions relating to several key areas appropriate for the direct interview. Most questions are open-ended requiring elaboration on your part. For example, you might be asked:

Indirect Questions

"How do you feel about working in a large organization?"

"Tell me about your management philosophy."

"I'm interested in learning more about your marketing ideas. Tell me what you think would be some good approaches to developing overseas markets during the next five years, especially considering the state of the dollar in today's international markets."

You might take several minutes responding to such questions. And your response may lead the interviewer into related areas of questioning which were relatively unplanned.

In the indirect interview you will be at center stage doing most of the talking. You may feel at greater ease during such an interview because you feel less pressure to come up with the "right answer" to specific questions.

> **How you converse may be just as important as what you say.**

But beware of getting too comfortable during such an interview. You are still being evaluated even though you are not answering a series of specific questions most commonly identified as key to the interview process. The interviewer may be looking for key analytical, problem-solving, and communication skills along with determining your style, personality, and philosophies. In such a situation, **how** you answer the questions and converse with the interviewer may be just as important as **what** you say.

Stress

All interviews are stressful for job applicants. Fortunately for you, few interviewers actually put candidates through a **stress interview**. But since they do occur on occasion, you need to know what one is so you can keep your cool if you find you are subjected to one.

Stress interviews may be conducted by one person or by a panel of interviewers who fire numerous questions at the candidate. The tone of voice may be threatening, questions are quickly fired at the candidate— allowing little time for reflection—and in some situations the inter- viewer(s) may disagree with the candidate or each other.

The purpose of a stress interview is to see how the applicant reacts in a stressful situation. Some employers use this method when interviewing for positions which require coping with on-the-job stress. A chief of security, for example, points out he always subjects potential officers to a stress interview. He's hard on them and his goal is to reduce an applicant—male or female—to tears. If he's successful however, the applicant is not hired. He wants people who can remain in control of themselves and stressful situations; he believes the stress interview gives some indication of how well the candidate will perform under stress.

Not always is the connection between the stress interview and the stressful job as obvious as the one indicated in our security chief's example. But many employers want employees who can work in a pressure filled atmosphere. While they can review the individual's past record to learn about how he or she handles stress, the stress interview becomes a useful simulation for actually viewing the candidate handling stress.

If you encounter a stress interview, simply understanding what is happening and why will help you through the interview. Try to keep calm; don't allow the interviewer to upset you; and be complete but concise and to the point in your answers. The barrage pace of questions hurled at you won't leave time for wandering responses.

If you don't handle stress well, or if you are uncertain how you would deal with a stressful situation, this may be a good time to study the subject. Several useful books are available on stress management. Most include self-assessment tests and exercises designed for lowering and controlling stress levels.

Who Pays the Expenses

If you are invited to an interview in your local community there is no question about who pays the relatively few expenses involved. You do. But these expenses should be minimal—a gallon or two of gasoline and perhaps a parking fee.

However, for some positions employers conduct nationwide searches in an attempt to attract the best qualified person for a job. This is most likely to occur for high level positions or those that require specialized skills and are difficult to fill.

If you are invited to an interview that will involve significant travel expenses—hotel accommodations and perhaps even an airfare—you need to clarify the responsibility for expenses before you make the trip. Arrangements vary with the employer picking up the expenses in some situations, the applicant paying in others. In some cases there may even be an agreement that if the applicant is not offered the position, or is offered the position and accepts, the employer pays. But if the applicant is offered the position and declines it, the applicant pays the expenses.

Knowing who will pay the expenses could influence whether or not you wish to go for the interview. If you really don't think you want a particular job, you will be less inclined to interview if you know you must pay the expenses if you are offered the job, but decline.

If you are invited to an out-of-town interview and the employer has not mentioned anything about expenses, you will have to seek clarification. One way of doing this is to ask, *"What is XYZ company's policy on handling the travel expenses for the interview?"* This should get a statement of company policy and give the information you need to decide whether or not to travel to the interview.

To Eat or Not to Eat

While most interviews take place in an office, not all do. If you find part or all of an interview being conducted while you are expected to eat—in a restaurant or someone's home—be careful. The first guideline is to be just alert as you would be in the office. Do not be lulled into a false sense of security by thinking the interview is over and you can now relax. You are still being observed just as carefully as ever—perhaps moreso.

We are reminded of a fellow who had nervously gone through a morning of interviews—a series of interviews with different people in the organization. As noontime approached, he was invited to go to lunch with two of the people with whom he had already interviewed. As the three crossed the street to the restaurant, Bob breathed a sigh of relief and indicated he was glad the interviews were over. He proceeded to act as if they were. He no longer gave thoughtful responses to questions and he seemed very opinionated. Indeed, the company associates got to see Bob as he really was and decided they didn't like what they saw. You are on stage until you take your exit. Don't forget your part.

> You are on stage until you take your exit.

The second guideline is to eat food that is easy to eat and in small portions. Try to avoid spaghetti, fried chicken, and bony fish. You probably won't be too hungry anyway, and you won't eat much because you will be talking most of the time. But be sure you direct your attention to your audience—not your food! Your social graces are particularly on display in such settings. Especially watch your table manners.

The same admonition of moderation concerns liquor. At noontime the best advice is to abstain—even if others have ordered a drink. They may be testing you, and going back to work (or more interviews) after even one drink is not advisable no matter how well you think you can handle it. If you are at an evening dinner or cocktail party, you have some leeway with this rule. If you don't drink, simply decline the cocktail—there is no need for an explanation. If you do drink and wish to have a cocktail along with others, then **one** is generally acceptable. No more tonight—no matter how many the rest of the group consume! If you are female, you are safe if you order a glass of white wine. Most men find this less objectionable for women than hard liquor. Some women may be offended by this advice, but now is the time to go after the job—not the inequities.

6

Network For Interviews

Getting an interview is a difficult task for many job seekers. Organizations and employers seem closed to outsiders. Competition for jobs is often keen. Rejections are a frequent fact of job search life. Employers are busy people who try to limit the number of candidates they will see. So what can you do to get a job interview for the job you want?

You must take positive action to ensure you will be interviewed by the right people for the right job. Indeed, there are certain secrets to getting an interview you should know about before embarking on this stage of your job search. The most important secret is the informational interview—a type of interview which can lead to high quality job interviews and offers. These interviews minimize rejections and competition as well as quickly open the doors to organizations and employers. If you want a job interview, you first need to understand the informational interview and how to initiate and use it.

Probability Approaches

For most people, getting an interview is a game of chance. You are hopeful, but the odds are against you. You look for new strategies and techniques that will turn the odds in your favor.

The two most common approaches for getting an interview are to:

1. Mail numerous copies of your resume to employers in the hope that someone will invite you to an interview (THE SHOTGUN APPROACH).

2. Phone employers or mail your resume with a cover letter in response to advertised job vacancies (THE RESPONSE AP-PROACH).

Both approaches are relatively passive activities primarily involving written, clerical, and mailing skills.

Blindly mailing resumes to hundreds of employers in the hope someone will interview you is a probability game with the odds always against you. Let's face it; few people get interviews and job offers through the mail. We don't mean to minimize the importance of writing resumes and letters. After all, if you mail enough of them, you may develop a few job leads by sheer luck. But don't expect more than 2% of blind mailings to result in some type of job lead. The chances of your resume and letter reaching someone who has a job vacancy waiting for you is slight.

> # Uncover jobs that will use your strengths.

Even if you are lucky with this shotgun approach, it will seldom yield high quality jobs. The very fact you are shotgunning your resumes and letters means you are trying to find a job you might fit into rather than one that is fit for you. You should uncover jobs that will use your strengths rather than locate jobs that may accentuate your weaknesses. To do otherwise means short-changing your chances of finding a job you will both do well and enjoy doing. Other approaches outlined in this book are more likely to move you closer to your goal.

Advertised and Hidden Job Markets

Most job hunters turn to the **advertised job market** for employment leads. This is a highly visible, relatively well structured, and coherent market consisting of job vacancy announcements in newspapers, trade journals, professional newsletters, employment agencies, and personnel offices. People look to these sources, because they are familiar with them, and because they believe the jobs available at any given time are listed in these places. However, these advertised sources may only identify 25% of job vacancies at any particular time.

So where do you find the other 75% of the job openings? Most jobs are found on the unadvertised and relatively unstructured, chaotic **hidden job market**. Here you will find job vacancies people know about because they hear what's going on in organizations or they know someone who is quitting or an employer has a need for a new employee. In addition to encompassing the largest proportion of available jobs, the hidden job market tends to yield the **highest quality jobs**. Best of all, you face the **least competition** and the **fewest rejections** in this job market. You gain access to this market by word-of-mouth—through friends, relatives, acquaintances, and informed strangers. Knowing this, it is to your advantage to concentrate most of your job search efforts on this relatively unstructured and unpublicized job market.

At the same time, you should monitor the advertised job market. You occasionally may find a job that you believe is right for you. If so, apply as you normally would with a resume and cover letter and follow-up with telephone calls. But you should not spend a great deal of your job search time working the publicized job listings. Unless you are exceptionally well qualified, you may waste a great deal of time and effort responding to such listings. Therefore, a good rule of thumb is to devote no more than 25% of your job search time in the advertised job market. Your time is best spent on higher pay-off activities aimed at the hidden job market.

Vacancies and Employers

Put yourself in the position of the employer for a moment. You have a job vacancy to fill. If you advertise the position, you may be bombarded with hundreds of applications, phone calls, and walk-ins. While you do want to hire the best qualified individual for the job, you simply don't have time nor patience to review scores of applications. Even if you use a P.O. Box number, the paperwork may be overwhelming. Furthermore, with limited information from application forms, cover letters, and resumes, you find it hard to identify the best qualified individuals to invite for an interview; many look the same on paper.

So what do you do? You might hire a professional job search firm to take on all of this additional work. On the other hand, you may want to better control the hiring process. Like many other employers, you begin by calling your friends, acquaintances, and other business associates and ask if they or someone else might know of any good candidates for the position. If they can't help, you ask them to give you a call should they know of anyone qualified for your vacancy. You, in effect, create your own hidden job market—an informal information network for locating desirable candidates. Your trusted contacts initially screen the candidates in the process of referring them to you.

Based on this understanding of the employer's perspective, what should you do to best improve your chances of getting an interview and job offer? Remember, the employer needs to solve a personnel problem. By conducting **informational interviews and networking** you help the employer solve his or her problem by giving them a chance to examine what you can offer them. You gain several advantages by conducting these interviews:

1. You are less likely to encounter rejections since you are not asking for a job—only information, advice, referrals, and to be remembered.

2. You go after higher level positions.

3. You encounter little competition.

4. You go directly to the people who have the power to hire.

5. You are likely to be invited to job interviews based upon the referrals you receive.

This job search approach has a much higher probability of generating job interviews and offers than the more traditional shotgunning and advertised job market approaches.

Minimize Rejections and Build Networks

Ask anyone who is about to embark on a job search what they fear most, and they will almost certainly answer "being rejected." None of us like to be told "no." Some of us fear rejections more than others. Yet the common method for seeking employment—responding to job listings—leaves the job searcher vulnerable to a host of "noes."

While you will encounter some "noes" in your search for "yeses," informational interviews minimize the number of "noes" you will collect. Using this approach, you seldom will be turned down for an interview. In fact, most people will be happy to share their experiences with you and give you information, advice, and referrals. More important, informational interviews help you overcome the likelihood of rejection.

The first rule in conducting informational interviews is to **never ask for a job**. When you ask for a job or ask to be interviewed for a job (which you do when you send off your resume), you set yourself up to receive a rejection. If no job is available, you put the employer in an uncomfortable position of telling you "no." If you apply for an advertised opening, you will probably get lost in the herd of applicants. On the other hand, if you request an interview for information and advice—not a job—you are likely to get a "yes."

> ## Informational interviews minimize the number of "noes" you will collect.

Informational interviews will help you build networks for locating the better jobs and careers. For example, look at the classifieds in your local newspaper. Most of the positions listed are either lower level positions or they require a high level of technical skills—in other words, positions that are difficult to fill. Since the jobs you learn about through your networks are often neither advertised nor competitive, your odds of getting a good job improve considerably. As you continue making new contacts through additional referrals, you will build a large network of job contacts. Individuals in your network will be your eyes and ears for locating job opportunities that are appropriate to your goals and skills.

Informational interviews remain one of your best job search strategies. However, because some job seekers have abused the entree informational interviews provide, you may find some employers more reluctant than they once were to open their door to strangers seeking employment advice. It will help if you have a referral—someone whom they know recommended that you call. If you have such a referral, make certain you mention the name of the person early in your letter or phone call.

Assure the employer that you have specific questions to address and will take a limited amount of their time. The employer may indicate she will answer questions on the phone but hasn't the time to see you in person. Obviously you would rather conduct a face-to-face informational interview. But take what you can get and in either case be truly appreciative. These are busy people whose time is valuable. Never use an informational interview as a guise for trying to get a job with this employer. Yes, sometimes it works out that way. People have gotten jobs through the informational interview, but that is the exception rather than the rule. You may find it more difficult to get informational interviews because of irresponsible people who have gotten there before you. But when you do land an informational interview, be prepared, be professional, and be appreciative.

Gather Career Information

As noted in Chapter 4, the first step—and often the most difficult one—in the job search is knowing what you do well and enjoy doing. Your goal is to find the job or career path which enables you to make a living using your strengths.

The informational interview gives you the opportunity to find out if a particular job or career is right for you. You gain valuable information for making career decisions by talking with individuals who work in your field of interest. These individuals will tell you what skills are necessary to perform the job and outline the realities—both advantages and disadvantages—of working in their field. It is best to learn about these things **before** you find yourself in a job you may not like but which appeared attractive in a job description.

Informational interviews can best be conducted by people at two different stages of their careers. Gaining information is useful to the student who has selected a career field and wishes to validate that choice, and make optimum choices to prepare for that career. Informational interviews are also valuable to the person embarking on an actual job search.

Gain Access

You will conduct informational interviews with different types of people. Some will be friends, relatives, or acquaintances. Others will be referrals or new contacts. You will gain the easiest access to people you already know. This can usually be done informally by telephone. You might meet at their home or office or at a restaurant.

You should use a more formal approach to gain access to referrals and new contacts. The best approach is to write an approach letter and follow up with a phone call. Examples of approach letters are found in Appendix A. Your approach letter should include the following elements:

Key Elements in the Approach Letter

OPENERS: If you have a referral, tell the individual you are considering a career in _____. His or her name was given to you by _____ who suggested he or she might be a good person to give you some useful information about careers in __ _____. If you lack a referral to the individual and thus must use a "cold turkey" approach to making this contact, you might begin your letter by stating that you are aware he or she has been at the forefront of _____ business—or whatever is both truthful and appropriate for the situation. A subtle form of flattery will be helpful at this stage.

REQUEST: Demonstrate your thoughtfulness and courtesy rather than aggressiveness by mentioning that you know he or she is busy. You hope to schedule a mutually convenient time for a brief meeting to discuss your career concerns. Most people will be flattered by such a request and will to talk with you about their work—if they have time and are interested in you.

CLOSINGS: In closing the letter, mention that you will call the person to see if an appointment can be arranged. Be specific by stating the time and day you will call—for example, Thursday at 2pm. You must take the initiative in this manner to follow-up the letter with a definite contact time. If you don't, you cannot expect to hear from the person. It is **your** responsibility to make the telephone call to schedule a meeting.

ENCLOSE: Do **not** enclose your resume with this approach letter. You should take your resume to the interview and present it as a topic of discussion near the end of your meeting. If you send it with the approach letter, you communicate a mixed and contradictory message. Remember your purpose for this interview: to gather information and advice. You are not—and never should be—asking for a job. A resume in a letter appears to be an application or a request for a job.

Formulate Questions

In the informational interview **you** are the interviewer. It is you who are primarily seeking information. Therefore, you need to think through, prior to the interview—whether by telephone or in person—several questions you want to probe. The following are examples of the kinds of questions you should ask. However these questions are only examples to help you begin thinking about what you need to know. Some questions are more appropriate to a college student trying to fine tune career decisions. Others are more appropriate to the individual ready to launch a job search. You should be able to generate additional questions that pertain to your situation.

Informational Interview Questions

- What type of skills and knowledge does one need to perform this job?

- What are some of the particular advantages and disadvantages of this type of work?

- What type of advancement opportunities are there?

- What is the future outlook like in this line of work?

- Could you describe a typical work day for me?

- What do you like about your work?

- What do you dislike about your work?

- What are the normal salary ranges for this type of work?

- What is the salary range for someone at my level of skills, education, and experience? (Entry-level or experienced)

- How would I best acquire the necessary skills for this job?

- What objections might employers have to my background?

- What employers would most likely hire someone for the job I am targeting?

- What do you think would be the best way for me to approach prospective employers?

- How did you go about finding this job?

Your initial questions should focus on how to improve your job search rather than gather information on the person's company. If, as the interview progresses, it seems appropriate to ask specific questions about the company, go ahead and ask; but be careful. Remember, you are **not** interviewing for a position with this company—**you are seeking information about a job or career in a given field.** You do not want to wear out your welcome by making the individual feel uncomfortable with questions about a job vacancy this person might have for you. And people do get uncomfortable when you start asking them for a job!

Conduct the Interview

If you approach people in the right manner, at least 50 percent of those you contact for informational interviews will meet with you. Some job hunters are never refused such an interview. Assuming you too are successful in scheduling these interviews, what do you do at the interview?

In the informational interview you are asking for four things from the individual you are meeting with:

- information
- advice
- referrals
- to be remembered

At the same time, you are trying to impress upon the people you are interviewing that you possess the essential ingredients for being an outstanding employee: competent, intelligent, honest, enthusiastic, and likeable. You do this by following the same advice on how to conduct a formal job interview which we outline in Chapters 7 through 10.

While the informational interview is relatively unstructured, it should follow a general pattern of questions and answers. The interview should take no more than 45 minutes. However, it may go much longer if your interviewee gets carried away in sharing his or her experiences and giving you advice. But plan to cover your questions in a 30 to 45 minute period.

For best results, the interview should go something like this. The interview will begin with a few minutes of small talk—the weather, traffic, mutual acquaintances, a humorous observation. Next, you should initiate the interview by emphasizing your appreciation:

> *Thank you again for taking time to see me today. I appreciate your willingness to speak with me about my career plans. It is a subject which is very important to me at this juncture of my life.*

Follow this statement with a re-statement of your purpose, as you mentioned it in your letter and/or over the telephone:

> *I am in the process of exploring several job and career alternatives. I know what I do well and enjoy doing. But before I make any decisions in this regard, I am trying to benefit from the counsel of individuals, such as you, who have a great deal of experience in the area of _____. I am particularly interested in learning more about opportunities, necessary skills, responsibilities, advantages, disadvantages, and the future outlook for this field.*

Such a general statement should elicit a response from the individual. It should put him or her at ease by stressing your need at this time for counsel rather than a job.

Be sure you communicate your purpose at this stage and that you know what you want to do. If you don't, the individual may feel you are wasting his or her time. Thus, your questions need to be focused. You need to know your strengths as well as have a clearly defined objective

prior to this interview.

The next section of the interview should focus on several "how" and "what" questions concerning specific jobs or careers:

- Duties and responsibilities
- Knowledge, skills, abilities, and qualifications
- Work environments—employees, deadlines, stress, problems
- Advantages and disadvantages
- Future outlook
- Salary ranges (in general and at your entry level)

Each of these questions can take a great deal of time to answer and discuss. Therefore, prioritize the ones you most need to ask, and try to keep the conversation moving on the various subjects.

Your second major line of questioning should center on your job search. Here you want to solicit useful advice for improving your job search. You now want to know how to:

- Acquire the required skills
- Find a job related to this field
- Overcome employers' objections to you
- Identify both advertised and unadvertised vacancies
- Develop new job leads
- Approach prospective employers

Your last major set of questions should deal with your resume. Remember, you have taken copies of your resume to this interview but the person has not seen your resume yet. You have done this purposefully to avoid giving the impression that you are using the informational interview to try to get a job. In addition, it gives the individual a chance to get to know you prior to seeing your paper qualifications. Now, near the end of the interview, you ask the person to critique your resume. Give him or her a copy and ask these questions:

Resume Review Questions

- Is this an appropriate type of resume for the jobs I have outlined?

- If an employer received this resume in the mail, how do you think he or she would react to it?

- What do you see as possible weaknesses or areas that need to be improved?

- What about the length, paper quality and color, layout, and typing? Are they appropriate?

- How might I best improve the form and content of the resume?

By doing this, the interviewee will be forced to read your resume—which is a good summary of what you talked about earlier in the interview. Most important of all, he or she will give you useful advice on how to improve and target your resume.

Your last two questions are actually requests to be **referred and remembered.** As you express your gratitude for the person's time, ask for referrals:

Thanks very much for all your assistance. I have learned a great deal today. Your advice will certainly help me give my job search better direction. I would like to ask one more favor. By conducting research on various jobs, I am trying to benefit from the counsel of several people. Do you know two or three other people who might be willing to meet with me, as you have today?

Express ideas similar to these—but in your own words. Do not try to memorize answers. Focus on the ideas you wish to convey and respond in a natural manner. If you try to memorize responses, they will sound "canned" and insincere. Just before you leave, ask to be **remembered** for future reference:

While I know you may not know of a job opening at present for someone with my qualifications, I would appreciate it if you could keep me in mind if you learn of any openings. Please feel free to pass my name on to anyone you feel might be interested in my qualifications.

Make sure you leave a copy of your resume with this person so that he or she has something tangible to refer to and remember you by.

After completing this interview, you should send a nice **thank you letter** to this person. Not only is this a thoughtful thing to do, it is also a wise thing to do if you wish to be remembered and referred. Genuinely express your gratitude for the person's time and help, and reiterate your wish to be remembered and referred. We've provided examples of thank you letters in Appendix B. Review these letters, but be sure you write ones reflecting **your** experience and feelings. Do **not** copy our examples.

As you conduct several of these informational interviews, you may want to keep records of each meeting. Use 4 x 6 index cards to record the name, date, and highlights of the interview. Be sure to include any names of referrals for future reference.

Information Quality and Usefulness

You will often get more honest information in an informational interview than in an employment interview. In trying to fill vacancies, employers cannot be objective because they also are attempting to sell you on the benefits of working for them. There is less pressure in informational interviews to be persuasive.

Informational interviews will help you determine if you are interested in a particular career field or job. For example, in our work with college students, we encounter many who aspire to become attorneys. However, a typical conception is based on seeing too many episodes of L.A. Law and Perry Mason. The image of legal work often is one of standing before the jury dramatically arguing a case. Once these students realize that the two most important skills attorneys use are research and counseling, many lose interest in this career field.

Conducting informational interviews can help you avoid jobs or careers that are not right for you. Whether you are looking forward to a job after you finish school or are already in the workforce but desire to make a job change, informational interviews are valuable tools.

Serendipity

When conducting informational interviews, you may occasionally uncover a job opening with the person you are interviewing. Sometimes the company may consider creating a position for you because they are so impressed with your credentials. We have seen this happen with individuals we have counseled. But these are exceptions rather than the rule. Do not go into an informational interview expecting to come out with anything more than information, advice, referrals, and the promise to be remembered.

Successful Networking and Interviewing

As you conduct informational interviews and network with many individuals, keep these four rules in mind:

Rules For Success

1. Look for a job that is fit for you rather than try to fit yourself into an available position.

2. Increase your number of acceptances by conducting informational interviews. When you ask for information, advice, and referrals, few people will turn you down. Most people you ask will be flattered and eager to assist you.

3. When conducting informational interviews, never ask for a job; always ask for information, advice, referrals, and to be remembered.

4. Always send a thank you letter.

If you follow these simple rules, your informational interviews may turn into actual job interviews which lead to job offers for high quality jobs. If you decide not to engage in networking and informational interviews, all is not lost. People do get interviews and jobs by submitting applications and resumes in response to job vacancy announcements. The difference is that you may have to spend a great deal of time on the inherently frustrating advertised job market where you are likely to experience high competition, numerous rejections, and a much lengthier job search process. But just as important, the information you gain from your informational interviews will help you when you find yourself in the actual job interview. You can deal much better with the question of salary, for example, if you have a clear idea what comparable jobs pay in your geographic area.

Our recommendation: try the networking and informational interviewing strategies outlined in this chapter. Trust us—they work wonders in today's competitive job market!

7

Prepare For Job Interviews

The best interviewees go to the interview well prepared. Approaching the job interview as the single most important step to getting the job, they get ready by:

- Reviewing their strengths and goals.
- Researching the organization.
- Anticipating the interviewer and the interview situation.
- Practicing strategies to answer anticipated questions with well thought-out responses.
- Compiling key questions they need to ask the interviewer.

Once in the interview, these interviewees try to be spontaneous while still in control of themselves and the interview situation. All else being equal, they interview better than their ill-prepared counterparts because (1) the content of the interview conveys they are intelligent and interested—the verbal cues, and (2) they feel more competent and exude greater self-assurance—the nonverbal cues.

When you conduct an informational interview, you are the **interviewer**. You now change roles and primarily become the **interviewee** in the job interview. As you do this, you must follow a new set of rules for effective interviewing. Our best advice: prepare, prepare, prepare. Prepare for the interview as if it were a $1,000,000 prize. Indeed, if you are hired, you may earn that much income during the years you are on the job!

Conduct Research

When preparing for an interview, you should first research the organization. In addition, try to conduct research on the individual or individuals who will be interviewing you. Obviously, the more you know about the organization prior to the interview, the more you will learn during the interview. You will be a more impressive candidate if you offer thoughtful answers and ask intelligent questions based on a knowledge of the employer.

How do you do research on the organization? If you already conducted an informational interview with someone in the organization, you will have acquired some useful information. If you happen to know other individuals in the organization—friends or acquaintances—contact them for information prior to your interview.

Information Sources and Questions

Your best information on organizations and the interviewer will come from conversations with people who are close to the organization, especially present and former employees. Hopefully, you have already met with these people in the process of conducting your informational interviews. Following the questions outlined in Chapter 6 for conducting effective informational interviews, you should have a solid basis upon which to anticipate answering and asking questions.

However, if you failed to conduct informational interviews or if you need additional information, several published sources are available to assist you. Most of them are available in the reference section of your local public or college library. Consult, for example, some of the following sources:

- *American Encyclopedia of International Information*
- *American Men and Women in Science*
- *American Register of American Manufacturers*
- *Bernard Klein's Guide to American Directories*
- *The College Placement Annual*
- *Directory of Professional and Trade Organizations*
- *Dun and Bradstreet's Middle Market Directory*
- *Dun and Bradstreet's Million Dollar Directory*
- *Encyclopedia of Associations*

- *Encyclopedia of Business Information Services*
- *Fitch's Corporation Reports*
- *MacRae's Blue Book—Corporate Index*
- *The Standard Periodical Directory*
- *Standard and Poor's Corporation Records: Register of Corporations, Directors, and Executives*
- *Standard and Poor's Industrial Index*
- *Standard Rate and Data Business Publications Directory*
- *Who's Who in America*
- *Who's Who in Commerce and Industry*
- *Who's Who in Finance and Industry*
- *Who's Who in the East*
- *Who's Who in the South*
- *Who's Who in the West*

Don't overlook useful information available on the Internet. Most companies, including small firms within your community as well as your local Chamber of Commerce, have home pages on the World Wide Web. These Web sites can be rich sources of information that can be accessed 24-hours a day.

Your **research** should address several questions which will yield useful information for the interview. Your first set of questions should relate to the organization:

Organization Questions

- Who are the key people in this organization?

- What are the major products or services produced by this organization?

- How large an organization is it in terms of both annual sales and employees?

- What is its profit and loss record for the past 10 years?

- Where is the company located other than in this community?

- How is the company organized?

- How is the company viewed by its clients, suppliers, and competition?

Another set of questions should center on the interviewer and the interview situation. You need to be better informed about the type of interview you will encounter:

Interview Situation Questions

- Who normally conducts the interview? Position? Male or Female? Age? Personality? Style?

- How many interviews will I likely go through with this organization before they make the final hiring decision?

- How many individuals or groups must I meet during the interview(s)?

- What type of interviews does this organization conduct? Electronic screening? One-on-one? Series? Panel? Group?

- What type of questioning techniques do they use? Direct? Indirect? Stress?

- Where will the interview(s) take place? Telephone? Airport? Hotel? Company office? Restaurant? Interviewer's home?

- Must I take any examinations? If so, what are they and how are they evaluated?

While these lists of questions will get you started, you should generate additional questions relevant to your goals and the particular job and company with which you will be interviewing.

Having information about the organization prior to the interview is important because most of the interview will undoubtedly center on the firm and how your skills and goals relate to it. However, in reality companies do not hire—people do. If possible, also learn something about the person or persons who will be conducting the interview. This information may be obtained from people you know within the organization, from promotional literature published by the firm, or from newspapers, magazines, or *Who's Who* books.

As we will note later, hiring decisions are not based solely on the candidate's competence. After all, everyone selected to be interviewed is thought to possess at least the basic qualifications. Equally important is how well the interviewer **likes** the candidate. Employers also want to know how well you will **fit into** the organization. In other words, how competent, intelligent, honest, enthusiastic and likable are you? Answers to these questions are at the bottom line of the hiring decision. Therefore, the more you know about your interviewer prior to the interview, the better you should be able to manage the interview.

> **Employers want to know how well you will fit into the organization.**

Refocus Your Goals and Strategies

We assume you have already identified your goals and strengths in the process of completing three key job search steps as outlined in Chapter 3: skills identification, objective setting, and resume writing. Now it's time to review and refocus your goals and strengths around the specific position you will be interviewing for. This involves more than just generating and synthesizing data on yourself. You must **target** it on specific organizations and positions.

You can begin doing this by first examining any information you have describing the job for which you will interview. Based on both your research and the job description, look for statements of duties, responsibilities, skills, education, and experience as well as any exams required of candidates for the position. Next, carefully review your goals and strengths as elaborated on the worksheets in Chapter Four for identifying your key achievements, work values, and job objective. Take another look at this information so you can refocus it around the specifics outlined for the position to achieve a **best fit** of your strengths in relation to the employer's needs. Begin doing this by answering these questions:

- How do my major strengths and work values relate to the skill requirements for this position?

- To what extent are my goals compatible with the objectives of this position and the mission of this organization?

- How can I best restate the description for this position as a statement of my goals and strengths?

As you begin refocusing in this manner, you will begin positioning yourself more closely with the specific position and organization. You should become more employer-centered in the process of thinking in these terms. Your next major concern will be to begin talking in the employer's language of organizational goals and expected performance.

Practice For Examinations

Many positions require some form of examination as part of the interview process. This may occur at the very beginning as an initial screening device to determine if you should go on to the question/ answer stage of the interview. Other examinations may take place after completing the question-answer stage or even during the interview.

Once you determine the "if," "what," and "when" of any examination requirements, you should immediately begin to prepare for the examination. If, for example, a job requires typing skills, you may have to take a typing test. Since you know such tests aim at determining your speed and accuracy, you know what to do: sit down at your typewriter and time your speed and review your accuracy so you will know exactly how well you will perform on the test as well as determine if you need to improve your performance **before** taking the examination.

The same is true for other types of job skills. If you must give a presentation of some kind, practice with a tape recorder as well as an audience of friends who can give you useful feedback for improving your delivery skills. If you must take a test to determine your reasoning, analytical, and problem-solving skills, you should consult several books in the reference section of your local library which have practice tests for assessing such skills.

The questions asked of you during the interview are a form of examination. These you can anticipate and consider appropriate answers. But other types of examinations usually involve specific performance criteria you need to know about and prepare for. If you don't do well on these tests, you cannot expect to pass the critical interview stage.

Prepare For Questions

Assuming you know yourself and have done all the necessary research for anticipating the interviewer and the interview situation, you next need to prepare for both general and specific interview questions. Although you cannot anticipate in advance the exact questions the interviewer will ask, you can anticipate the general lines of inquiry. You can expect to be asked questions regarding your education, your work experience, your career goals, and how you get along with others. Many questions will be historical in nature. They probe your background. Several of these questions will certainly arise during the interview:

Anticipated Questions

Your Education

- Describe your educational background.
- Why did you attend _____ University (or College)?
- Why did you major in _____ ?
- What was your grade point average?
- What subjects did you enjoy the most? The least? Why?
- What leadership positions did you hold?
- How did you finance your education?
- If you were to start over, what would you change about your education?
- Why were your grades so low? So high?
- Did you do the best you could in school? If not, why not?

Your Work Experience

- What were your major achievements in each of your past jobs?
- Why did you change jobs before?
- What is your typical workday like?
- What functions do you enjoy doing the most?
- What did you like about your boss? Dislike?
- Which job did you enjoy the most? Why? Which job did you enjoy the least? Why?
- Have you ever been fired? Why?

Your Career Goals

- Why do you want to join our organization?
- Why do you think you are qualified for this position?
- Why are you looking for another job?
- Why do you want to make a career change?
- What ideally would you like to do?
- Why should we hire you?
- How would you improve our operations?
- What is the lowest pay you will take?
- How much do you think you are worth for this job?
- What do you want to be doing five years from now?
- How much do you want to be making five years from now?
- What are your short-range and long-range career goals?
- If you could choose your job and organization, where would you go?
- What other types of jobs are you considering? Other companies?
- When will you be ready to begin work?
- How do you feel about relocating, traveling, working overtime, and spending weekends in the office?
- What attracted you to our company?

Your Personality and Other Concerns

- Tell me about yourself.
- What are your major weaknesses? Your major strengths?
- What causes you to lose your temper?
- What do you do in your spare time? Any hobbies?
- What types of books do you read?
- What role does your family play in your career?
- How well do you work under pressure? In meeting deadlines?
- Tell me about your management philosophy.
- How much initiative do you take?
- What types of people do you prefer working with?
- How _____ (creative, analytical, tactful, etc.) are you?
- If you could change your life, what would you do differently?
- Who are your references?

In addition to these general areas of inquiry, ask yourself what other questions the interviewer might ask given your particular background, resume, and references. For example:

- Do you have any time gaps that are unaccounted for in your work or educational history?

- Have you held several jobs or attended several schools in a relatively short time span?

- Does your work history show a pattern of lateral (or downward) movement within or between organizations?

- Are you applying for a job with less responsibility/pay than your present or most recent job?

Behavioral Questions

More employers are asking behavior based questions these days. This comes from the belief that how a job candidate has responded to certain types of situations in the past is a good predictor of how that person will behave in a similar future situation. Behavior based questions are likely to begin with some variation of:

- Give me an example of time when . . .
- Give me an example of how you . . .
- Tell me about how you . . .

This is an opportunity for you to sell your positives with an example or two. Briefly describe the situation, enthusiastically explain what you did (adding information as to why if you think this would not be evident), and indicate the outcome.

For example, if the interviewer asks,

"Tell me about a time when you saved an account for your company."

The applicant might respond,

"Just last month I was observing a one-day training session conducted by one of our instructors I supervise. His class evalua-

tions were lower than what we expect of our trainers and my boss told me the client was not happy with the way the training sessions were going. He was afraid we might lose the account.

As I observed the session it was apparent the instructor knew the material but was having trouble moving the participants through the material in the time allotted. They often broke into small groups to complete an activity, but it was taking a long time as some groups had to wait for others to finish. At the end of the day Joe and I met with the client who indicated his dissatisfaction and gave us an ultimatum: if the training of future groups couldn't be completed in a day and to his satisfaction, he would get another contractor.

I solved the problem by having Joe develop copies of the end product the participants should have formulated at the end of each segment of the activity. At the next training session he was able to pass these out at the end of the allotted time for each phase of the activity.

The seminar participants understood the information and gave the instructor excellent course evaluations and the client was pleased. We not only saved this contract, but got an additional contract from the client as well. My boss and I were both pleased with the outcome."

Obviously you want to select examples that promote your skills and have a positive outcome. Even if the interviewer asks about a time when something negative happened, try to select an example where you were able to turn the situation around and something positive came out of it. For example, if asked, *"Tell me about a time you made a bad decision."* Try to identify an example where:

- even though it wasn't the best decision, you were able to pull something positive out of the situation

- though it was a poor decision, you learned from it and in the next similar situation you made a good decision or know how you will handle it differently the next time a similar situation arises

- it was bad decision but the negative outcome had only minor impact

In other words, try to pull something positive—either that you did or that you learned—out of even a negative experience you are asked to relate. The employer is interested in the process you went through and the reasoning behind your actions—not just the outcome. As you prepare for your interview, consider situations where you:

- demonstrated leadership
- solved a problem
- increased company profits
- made a good decision/made a poor decision
- handled change (not money, but changing events)
- handled criticism
- met a deadline/missed a deadline
- worked as part of a team

Add to this list other behavioral questions you think of that apply to the job for which you are applying. For example, if the job includes making presentations, expect questions about a speech where you achieved your goal or conversely about a time when your speech failed miserably.

Ask others who have interviewed with the company, if possible, what types of questions to expect. You may encounter hypothetical questions in which you are asked not what you did, but what you would do *if* something occurred. With hypothetical questions the interviewer is usually not interested so much in your actual answer—often there is no correct or incorrect response—as in your thought process. The information is in how you would solve a problem or respond to a particular type of situation.

Anticipate questions you might be asked so you can prepare a well thought-out response prior to the interview. Be ready to give examples and details of what you did (process) and what happened (outcome). You need to be able to back up your assertions with support. Go to the interview prepared with examples, statistics, and testimonials. When asked how you handled a situation, you have examples ready to relate. When you assert that your re-organization of a department resulted in improved customer service, you can back this up by indicating that customer complaints decreased by 55 percent after you instituted changes. When you tell that you were a star salesperson, you can add that your company recognized you with the first place sales award two years in a row. Be prepared to answer the interviewer's questions with a truthful, yet positive pitch and then support your pitch with examples, illustrations, statistics, or testimonials. It is far easier to formulate positive responses to questions in the relaxed setting of your living room than in the stressful and time constrained setting of the job interview.

Illegal Questions and Tactful Responses

Title VII of the Civil Rights Act of 1964 makes discrimination on the basis of race, sex, religion, or national origins illegal in personnel decisions. Questions that delve into these areas as well as others, such as age, height, or weight, are also illegal, unless they can be shown to directly relate to bona fide occupational qualifications. Most interviewers are aware of these restrictions and avoid asking such questions. However, you may still encounter such questions either because of ignorance on the part of the interviewer or blatant violation of the regulation.

Women are more likely to face illegal questions than men. Some employers still ask questions regarding birth control, child care, or how their husbands feel about them working or traveling. The following types of questions are considered illegal:

Illegal Questions

- Are you married, divorced, separated, or single?
- How old are you?
- Do you go to church regularly?
- Do you have many debts?
- Do you own or rent your home?
- What social or political organizations do you belong to?
- What does your spouse think about your career?
- Are you living with anyone?
- Are you practicing birth control?
- Were you ever arrested?
- How much insurance do you have?
- How much do you weigh?
- How tall are you?

Although we hope you will not encounter these types of questions during your job search, you should consider how you would handle them if they arise. Your decision should be thought out carefully beforehand rather than made in the stressful setting of the interview. It must be your decision—one that you feel comfortable with.

You may want to consider the following suggestions as options for handling illegal and personal questions. If you encounter such questions, your choice may depend upon which is more important to you: defending a principle or giving yourself the greatest chance to land the job. You may decide the job is not as important as the principle. Or you may decide, even though you really want this job, you could never work in the organization that employed such clods, and tell them so.

On the other hand, you may decide to answer the question, offensive though it may be, because you really want the job. If you get the job, you vow you will work from within the organization to change such interview practices.

There is yet a third scenario relating to illegal questions. You may believe the employer is purposefully trying to see how you will react to stressful questions. Will you lose your temper or will you answer m-eekly? Though a rather dangerous practice for employers, this does occur nonetheless. In this situation you should remain cool and answer tactfully by indicating indirectly that the questions may be inappropriate. For example, if you are divorced and the interviewer asks about your divorce, you could respond by asking, *"Does a divorce have a direct bearing on the responsibilities of _____?"* If the interviewer asks if you are on the pill, you could respond, *"Yes, I take three pills a day—vitamins A, B, and C, and because of them, I haven't missed a day's work in the past year."* The interviewer should get the message, and you will have indicated you can handle stressful questions.

> # Turn what appears to be a negative into a positive.

A possible response to any illegal question—regardless of motive—is to turn what appears to be a negative into a positive. If, for example, you are female and the interviewer asks you how many children you still have living at home and you say, *"I have five—two boys and three girls,"* you can expect this answer will be viewed as a negative vis a vis employment. Working mothers with five children at home may be viewed as neither good mothers nor dependable employees. Therefore, you should immediately follow your initial response with a tactful elaboration that will turn this potential negative into a positive. You might say,

*I have five—two boys and three girls. They are wonderful children
who, along with my understanding husband, take great care of
each other. If I didn't have such a supportive and caring family,
I would never think of pursuing a career in this field. I do want
you to know that I keep my personal life separate from my
professional life. That's very important to me and my family, and
I know it's important to employers. In fact, because of my family
situation, I make special arrangements with other family members,
friends, and day-care centers to ensure that family responsibilities
never interfere with my work. But more important, I think being a
mother and working full-time has really given me a greater sense
of responsibility, forced me to use my time well, and helped me
better organize my life and handle stress. I've learned what's
important in both my work and life. I would hope that the fact that
I'm both a mother and I'm working—and not a working mother—would be something your company would be supportive of,
especially given my past performance and the qualifications I
would bring to this job.*

Here you were able to take both an illegal question and a potential
negative and turn them into a positive—perhaps the most tactful and
effective way of dealing with a situation other interviewees might
respond to in a negative manner.

You should decide before you go into the interview how you will
handle similar situations. If you are prepared for possible illegal
questions, you may find your answers to such questions to be the
strongest and most effective of the interview!

Ask the Right Questions

As you prepare for the interview, you should outline questions you want
to ask the prospective employer. You need to ask questions to elicit
information **you** need about the position and organization; indeed, you
want to know if the position is fit for you. In addition, the interviewer
will be making judgments about your interests, qualifications, personality, and competence based on the number and types of questions you ask.

What types of questions should you ask in order to get information
and impress the interviewer? In general, questions relating to job duties,
responsibilities, opportunities for training, and employee advancement

within the company are appropriate. As we will note in Chapter 11, avoid asking self-centered questions. Those dealing with salary and benefits should be avoided during initial interviews or early stages of the interview unless they are raised first by the interviewer. Of course you are interested in salary, but you do not want to create the impression it is your primary concern. Remember, the prospective employer is interested in what **benefits** you will bring to the organization. At the same time, you need to **establish your value** in the eyes of the employer prior to discussing money.

The following set of questions outline some of the most common questions interviewees should ask. Again, do not consider this to be an exhaustive list, but use it to generate additional questions appropriate for your situation:

Questions You Should Ask

- What duties and responsibilities does the job entail?
- Where does this position fit into the organization?
- Is this a new position?
- What kind of person are you looking for?
- When was the last person promoted?
- What is the best experience and background for this position?
- Whom would I report to? Tell me a little about these people. Are you happy with them? What are their strengths and weaknesses?
- May I talk with present and previous employees about this job and organization?
- What problems might I expect to encounter on this job? (efficiency, quality control, declining profits, internal politics, evaluation)
- What has been done recently in regards to _____ ?
- What is the normal pay range for this job?
- How did you get your job?
- How long have you been with this company?
- Tell me about promotions and advancement with this company.
- What are your expectations from the person hired for this job?

Having prepared a written list of questions, many interviewees wonder whether they should memorize them or write them down and take them to the interview. We suggest writing them on an index card and carrying the card in your suit pocket, attache case, or purse. If, as the interview progresses, you remember all the questions you wished to ask without reference to the card, that is excellent. On the other hand, you may find you simply can't recall those questions—especially given the stress of the situation. If that happens, mention to the interviewer that you have some questions you want to be sure you don't forget to ask, and then refer to your index card. By formulating questions prior to the interview, you demonstrate concern about the position as well as preparation for the interview. Most interviewers will view you in a positive manner if you do this.

Practice the Interview

You have prepared for the interview by formulating your questions and answers. Once you have done this, you may wish to take advantage of some on-line resources designed to help individuals select appropriate answers to interview questions. Two popular sites on the Internet provide sample questions. E-span's site includes several multiple choice questions which are keyed to appropriate answers. You can explore this site at

http://www.espan.com/docs/intprac.html

The Student Center also includes an interview practice section. This one, however, is interactive; it provides feedback in the form of analysis for each answer you choose, whether correct or incorrect. You can examine this site at

http://www.studentcenter.com/brief/virtual/virtual.htm

You may wish to prepare even further by actually practicing the interview. There are several ways to do this. One method, requiring the least effort, is just to think through a hypothetical interview by anticipating questions, generating the jist your answers would take, and formulating questions you would ask. Another method is to have your spouse or a friend run you through a practice interview. Give them a list of questions in order to role play the interviewer-interviewee encounter. Another method is to tape record—either on your own or with a friend—interview questions and responses. By doing this, you will be able to evaluate your effectiveness in handling interview questions. Review your recording and repeat questioning and responding until you are pleased with the results. Don't try to memorize responses. You should not try to say the same thing in the same way each time. Chances are if you memorize, your responses will sound "canned." Your goal should be to convey the message with the meaning you intend in a manner that seems comfortable and spontaneous. Practice getting the intent across, but expect that you will say it somewhat differently each time.

Preparation for the interview takes time and hard work. Since our focus is on successful interviewing, we have no quick and easy methods for getting the job you want. When you go into the office for the job interview, you know you are competing with others who may be just as well qualified as you. At this point the slate is wiped clean; you and the other candidates start from zero. Whether you or someone else is offered the position will largely depend upon the interviews—yours and theirs. As the door closes behind you, you'll be glad you took the time and effort to be well prepared for what could well become a $1,000,000 prize!

Review Your Preparation

As soon as you learn you are invited to a job interview, you should quickly assemble all the information you need, organize it around the specific position, and prepare for the major stages of the interview. Begin by reviewing our checklist of the most important elements that should go into preparing for your interview.

Your Interview Preparation Checklist

❏ Reviewed my research files on this organization.

❏ Conducted additional research on the organization, interview process, and interviewer to determine what I will encounter on the day of the interview.

❏ Refocused my goals and strengths around the job description.

❏ Answered all the organizational research questions I need to for this interview.

❑ Answered all the interview situation questions I need to for this interview.

❑ Identified what examinations I will have to take and prepared accordingly.

❑ Developed and rehearsed general answers to anticipated interview questions with a friend or/and used a tape recorder.

❑ Formulated a list of questions I need to ask the interviewer.

If you follow these interview preparation guidelines, you will be in a good position to handle most interview situations, interviewers, and questions. You should do well in communicating your strengths to employers.

8

Begin the Interview

Consider the implications of research findings for your job interviews. Studies indicate that if the interviewer forms a negative impression of the job applicant within the first five minutes of the interview, 90% of the time the individual is not hired. If the impression is positive during the initial five minutes, 75% of the time the person will be offered the job.

Critical Impressions

Impressions formed during the first two to six minutes of the interview are seldom changed during the remaining 30 to 60 minutes of the interview. The maxim *"you never get a second chance to make a good first impression"* is one worth repeating.

Many people still believe the best qualified person always gets the job. But we act and react to situations based on our perceptions of reality and thus our perceptions become our reality. The same is true with interviewers. The most qualified individual is the one who **convinces** the interviewer that he or she—and not others—is the best qualified.

As we noted earlier, individuals invited to an interview have already been screened for basic job qualifications. Thus each interviewee is likely to possess the educational and work experience that are considered necessary for the job. At this point the person who gets the job is the one who impresses the interviewer as being the best for the job. And it is in those critical first few minutes where impressions count the most.

Win Points With a Positive Image

Appearance is the first thing you communicate to others. Before you have a chance to speak, others notice how you dress and accordingly draw conclusions about your personality and competence. Indeed, research shows that appearance makes the greatest difference when an evaluator has little information about the other person. This is precisely the situation you find yourself in at the start of the interview. In fact, if your appearance is not up to par, you may not even get to the interview. Employment counselors tell us that they meet with many applicants—both for temporary and permanent positions—that dress so inappropriately for a business setting that they cannot even send them on interviews with prospective employers even though their skills would make them viable candidates.

Many people object to having their capabilities evaluated on the basis of their appearance and manner of dress. *"But that is not fair," they argue. "People should be hired on the basis of their ability to do the job—not on how they look."* But debating the lack of merit or complaining about the unfairness of such behavior does not alter reality. Like it or not, people do make initial judgments about others based on their appearance. Since you cannot alter this fact and bemoaning it will get you nowhere, it is best to learn to use it to your advantage. If you learn to effectively manage your image, you can convey marvelous messages regarding your authority, credibility, and competence.

> **The most qualified individual convinces the interviewer he/she is the most qualified.**

Some estimates indicate that as much as 65 percent of the hiring decision may be based on the nonverbal aspects of the interview. Employers sometimes refer to this phenomenon with such terms as "chemistry," "body warmth," or that "gut feeling" the individual is right for the job. This correlates with findings of communication studies that approximately 65 percent of a message is communicated nonverbally. The remaining 35 percent is communicated verbally.

Rules of the Game

Knowing how to dress appropriately for the interview requires knowing important rules of the game. Like it or not, employers play by these rules. Once you know the rules, you at least can make a conscious choice whether or not you want to play. If you decide to play, you will stand a better chance of winning by using the often unwritten rules to your advantage.

Much has been written on how to dress professionally, especially since John Molloy first wrote his books on dress for success in the 1970s. While this approach has been criticized for promoting a "cookie cutter" or "carbon copy" image, it is still valid for most interview situations. The degree to which employers adhere to these expectations, however, will depend on particular individuals and situations. Your job is to know when, where, and to what extent the rules apply to you. When in doubt, follow our general advice on looking professional.

When we suggest you should know the rules and decide whether you wish to play by these rules, we do not intend to imply that incompetent people get jobs simply by dressing the part. Rather, we contend that qualified and competent job applicants can **gain an extra edge** over a field of other qualified, competent individuals by dressing to convey positive professional images.

Winning the Game

Much of the general advice on how to dress for success is sound. However, there is a major shortcoming in much of the advice you encounter. Researchers on the subject have looked at how people in positions of power view certain colors for professional attire. Few have gone beyond this to note that colors do different things on different people. Various shades or clarities of a color or combinations of contrast between light and dark colors when worn together may be unenhancing to some individuals and actually diminish that person's "power look."

For example, the combination of a white shirt or blouse paired with a navy suit—one of the success and power looks promoted by many— will be enhancing both to the appearance and the image of power on some individuals, but will be unenhancing and actually overpower the appearance of others. Or suppose you take the advice that a medium to charcoal gray suit is a good color in the professional world. It is, but the advice to wear medium to charcoal gray only recognizes differences of light to dark. In that medium to charcoal range we could pick scores of shades of gray from very blue grays to taupe grays. The wrong gray shade on individuals can make them look less attractive, unhealthy, and even older than their age. Who wants to hire someone who appears to be in poor health?

If we combine the results of research on how colors relate to one's power look and that done by JoAnna Nicholson and Judy Lewis-Crum explained in their book *Color Wonderful* on how colors relate to us as unique individuals, we can achieve a win-win situation. You can retain your individuality and look your most enhanced while, at the same time, achieving a look of success, power and competence.

Your Winning Appearance

The key to effective dressing is to know how to relate the clothing you put on your body to your own natural coloring. Both men and women can benefit from knowing how to make color work with—rather than against—their natural coloring. Let's pose a few questions to help you start thinking about color in what may be some new ways. Ask yourself:

- Can I wear black and white together and look good, or does that much contrast wear me?

- Can I wear navy and white together and retain my "power look" or does that much contrast actually diminish my look of power and authority?

- Can I wear a pure white or is a slightly cream toned white more flattering?

- Do I look better in clear or toned down shades of colors?

- Do I look better in a blued gray, a taupe gray, or a shade in between?

- Do I look better in a gold toned beige/camel, a cream toned beige/camel or a pink toned beige/camel color?

The answers to these questions vary with each individual and their own natural coloring. So it is important to know what the appropriate answers are for you.

Into which category does your coloring fit? Let's find out where you belong in terms of color type as classified by Color 1.

Identifying Your Color Type

- **Contrast coloring:** If you are a contrast color type, you have a definite dark-light appearance. You have very dark brown or black hair and light to medium ivory or olive toned skin. Black men and women in this category will have clear light to dark skin tones and dark hair.

- **Light-Bright coloring:** If you are of this color type, you have golden tones in your skin and golden tones in your blond or light to medium brown hair. Most of you had blond or light brown hair as children. Black men and women in this category will have clear golden skin on their face and dark hair.

- **Muted coloring:** If you are a muted color type, you have a definite brown-on-brown or red-on-brown appearance. Your skin tone is an ivory-beige, brown-beige, or golden-beige tone—that is, you have a beige skin with a golden-brown cast. Your hair could be red or light to dark brown with camel, bronze, or red highlights. Black men and women in this category will have golden or brown skin tones and dark hair.

- **Gentle coloring:** If you are of this color type, you have a soft, gentle looking appearance. Your skin tone is a light ivory or pink-beige tone and your hair is ash blond or ash brown. You probably had blond or ash brown hair as a child. Black men and women in this category will have pink tones in their skin and dark hair.

Some individuals may be a combination of two color types. If your skin tone falls in one category and your hair color in another, you are a combination color type.

The four basic color types will be referred to in the next two sections when guidelines are given for effectively combining shirts, suits, and ties for men, and skirted suits, blouses, and accessories for women to both enhance and maximize each individual's professional look.

However, if you are uncertain which hair or skin tone is yours and are hence undecided as to which color type category you belong to, you may wish to contact Color 1 Associates, Inc. by calling their toll free number: 1-800-523-8496. They can refer you to the Color 1 consultant nearest you. Color 1 provides the client with an individualized color chart that allows him/her to wear every color in the spectrum, but in their best **shade** and **clarity** as well as written material telling how to combine colors for the best amounts of contrast for one's natural coloring (color type).

A good color chart is an excellent one-time investment considering the costs of buying the wrong shade in a suit, shirt, or blouse. It will more than pay for itself if it contributes to an effective interview as you wear your suit in your best shade and put your clothing together to work with, rather than against, your natural coloring. It can help you convey positive images during those crucial initial minutes of the interview—as well as over a life-time.

Male Images of Success

John Molloy has conducted extensive research on how individuals can dress effectively. Aimed at individuals already working in professional positions who want to communicate a success image to further advancement, his advice is just as relevant for someone interviewing for a job.

Except for some blue collar jobs, basic attire for men interviewing for a position is **a suit**. Let's look at appropriate suits in terms of color, fabric, and style. The suit color can make a difference in creating an image of authority and competence. In general, blue, gray, camel or beige are proper colors for men's suits. Usually the darker the shade, the greater amount of authority it conveys to the wearer. Given your situation (the interview) and your audience (the interviewer), you should aim at conveying enough authority to command attention and a positive regard, but not so much as to threaten the interviewer. Hence, the **medium to charcoal gray or navy blue** would be good suit colors. Black, a basic funeral or formal attire color, can threaten the interviewer by conveying too much authority.

When selecting your gray, navy, camel, or beige suit, choose a shade that is enhancing to you. Should you wear a blue-gray, a taupe-gray, or a shade in-between? Do you look better in a somewhat bright navy or a more toned-down navy; a blue navy or a black navy; a navy with a purple or a yellow base to it?

In general, most people will look better in somewhat **blue grays** than in grays that are closer to the taupe side of the spectrum. Most people will be enhanced by a navy that is not too bright or contain so much black that it is difficult to distinguish whether the color is navy or black. When selecting a beige or a camel, select a tone that complements your skin color. If your skin has pink tones, avoid beiges and camels that contain gold hues and select pink based beiges/camels that enhance your skin color. Similarly, those of you who have gold/olive tones to your skin should avoid the pink based camels and beiges. If you are going to spend a lot of money on a suit—and if you buy a good, well-made suit you are going to spend a lot of money—buy a suit that will work for you.

Your suit(s) should be made of a **natural fiber**. A good blend of a natural fiber with some synthetic is acceptable as long as it has the "look" of the natural fiber. The very best suit fabrics are wool, wool blends, or fabrics that look like them. Even for the warmer summer months, men can find summer weight wool suits that are comfortable and look marvelous. They are your best buy. For really hot climates, a good silk (often blended with other materials) sport jacket is an acceptable choice when you choose not to wear a suit. A carefully chosen sport jacket is appropriate for many interview situations. Know however, that it conveys less authority than a suit. There may be times when you purposefully select this slightly less powerful—yet professional—look. Know your audience and make your decision accordingly.

The style of your suit should be **classic**. It should be well-tailored and well-styled. Avoid suits that appear "trendy" unless you are applying for a job in a field such as arts or some areas in advertising. A conservative suit that has a timeless classic styling will serve you best not only for the interview, but it will give you several years wear once you land the job.

John Molloy's New Dress For Success goes into great detail on shirts, ties, and practically everything you might wear or carry with you. It is not only instructive and up-to-date but makes enjoyable reading.

As you combine your clothing keep in mind **your color type**. If you have contrast or light-bright coloring, you will look great wearing your shade of white in a shirt with your navy blue shade in a suit. But if you have muted or gentle coloring, this is too much contrast for you. For muted or gentle coloring, the combination of navy and white will visually overpower you and you will not look your most enhanced.

If you are a muted or gentle color type, the look that gives you the greatest power look and yet does not overpower you will be a suit in your most flattering shade of gray worn with a shirt in your shade of white. You can expect your white to be less of a "pure" white (a bit more creamy—but not beige) than the white a contrast or a light-bright would wear. When you wear a navy suit, pair it with a blue shirt rather than a white one. This combines your colors in a level of contrast effective for your coloring.

Female Images of Success

Few men would consider wearing anything other than a suit to a job interview—especially an interview for a managerial or professional position. In the past, women have been less certain what is appropriate. As a result of research conducted by John Molloy and others, the verdict is now in. A skirted suit is the definite choice for the interview. This attire allows a woman to best convey images of professionalism, authority, and competence. Wearing a skirted suit can initially help a woman overcome negative stereotypes that some men still hold toward women in managerial and other professional positions.

Let's survey appropriate suits in terms of color, fabric, and style. As in the case of men's suits, the color of your suit can help create an image of authority and competence. The suit colors that make the strongest positive statements to enhance your power quotient are your shade of gray in a medium to charcoal depth or your shade of blue in a medium to navy depth of color. Plum, maroon and deep teal also test well. In general, a deep color conveys power and authority and neutrals such as beige and camel are conservative and acceptable in any business. You may wish to avoid black, however, which can convey so much authority in a business suit that many interviewers find it threatening.

When selecting your gray, navy, beige, or any other colored suit, follow the same rules we outlined for men: choose a shade that is enhancing to you. Women have more latitude than men in selecting colors for their business suits. Although dark colors do convey the greatest amount of authority to the wearer, you do not always need or want to select your most powerful colors. You may purposefully choose to wear one of your most flattering shades of red in a suit because you believe red will focus people's attention on you or cause you to be remembered. Or you may select your most flattering beige or camel for an interview where you don't want your most powerful look, but do wish to project a professional and conservative image. Remember to analyze your situation—the company where you are interviewing, the person(s) conducting the interview, as well as the position for which you are interviewing, and make a conscious choice as to the image you believe will best work for you. If you are uncertain which shades of all colors as well as neutrals are best for you, contact a Color 1 Associate for advice.

Similar to men's suits, your suit should be made of a **natural fiber** or have the "look" of a natural fiber. The very best winter-weight suit fabrics are wool or wool blends. For the warmer climates or the summer months, women will find few, if any, summer weight wool suits made for them. Hence linen, blended with a synthetic so it will not look as if it needs constant pressing, or a textured silk are good choices. Other fabrics, such as polyester blended with rayon, in clothing of good quality often has the definite look of linen but without the hassles of caring for real linen. But the key word here is **quality**. A cheap polyester/rayon fabric will look just that.

Your suit style should be **classic**. Following similar rules as for men, women's interview suits should be well-tailored, well-styled, and avoid a "trendy" look unless appropriate for certain occupations. A conservative, classic suit will last for years and is an excellent investment. Indeed, you can afford to buy good quality clothing if you know you will get a lot of use from the item. When deciding on your professional wardrobe, always buy clothes to last and buy quality.

Quality also means buying **silk blouses** if you can afford them. Keep in mind not only the price of the blouse itself, but the cleaning bill. There are many blouse fabrics that have the look and feel of silk on the market today. Silk or a fabric that has the look and feel of silk should be your choice for blouses to go with your business suits. Choose your blouses in your most flattering shades and clarity of color.

Although the skirted suit is the most professional look you can select, if you believe the situation calls for a professional, yet somewhat less authoritative look, you may choose to wear a conservatively tailored dress either with or without a jacket. But be certain you have carefully analyzed your interview situation before you take this option.

A popular look today combines a plaid suit jacket with a solid skirt and blouse that match one another and one of the jacket colors. Although a bit less powerful than the matched jacket and skirt, it can be a great look for the applicant and a refreshing change for an employer used to seeing similar outfits on all the applicants being interviewed. By putting the plaid jacket over a solid color blouse and skirt that match each other in color and are of one of the colors that predominate in the plaid of the jacket, you form a base for the plaid jacket that conveys both a flattering and professional look. Although it works well to use a plaid jacket that incorporates a predominate color that is the same as the base color you have chosen, it is not necessary. You can pair a solid color jacket over a solid color base if they coordinate well.

Remember to keep in mind **your color type**. Contrast or light-bright color types look great wearing their shade of white in a blouse with their navy blue shade in a suit. Muted or gentle color types will find this to be too much contrast and thus overpower their natural coloring. Such a color combination actually diminishes their power look.

If you are a muted or gentle color type, why not try your coral red shade blouse with your navy suit or wear a base of navy with a coral red jacket. Once you are aware of your color type and how to best enhance it while retaining visual authority, you will find many new and flattering combinations.

Give your outfit a more "finished and polished" look by **accessorizing** it effectively. Collect silk scarves and necklaces of semi-precious stones in your suit colors. For your suits comprised of a matching jacket and skirt, wear scarves, pins or necklaces in such a way that they repeat the color of the suit. For example, a woman wearing a navy suit and a red silk blouse could accent the look by wearing a necklace of navy sodalite beads, a pin of lapis lazuli or a silk scarf that has navy as a predominate color. If you form a base by wearing a matching solid color blouse and skirt with a plaid suit jacket, you have a choice of accessorizing with a gold or silver necklace or a necklace or solid color scarf using one of the jacket colors.

The most appropriate shoe to wear with a business suit is a **classic pump**—closed heel and toe with little or no decoration. Not only does this shoe stand by itself as creating the most professional look, it also teams best with a business suit and is flattering at the same time. An open-toe shoe or a sling-back can be worn with a suit, but will slightly diminish the wearer's professional look. Avoid shoes with both the heel and toe open as well as any sandal look. They can be beautiful shoes, but save them for evening wear. We have observed many women arriving for job interviews wearing suits, but ruining their professional image by wearing strappy sandal shoes. A thin strappy sandal look in a shoe does not have the visual weight to balance a suit. In general, wear shoes as dark or darker than your skirt. If not, you may draw the other person's eyes to your feet when, instead, you want them to focus on your face and on what you say.

You may choose to carry a **purse or an attache case**, but it is difficult to gracefully carry both at the same time. It is difficult not to look clumsy trying to handle both a purse and an attache case, and it is likely to diminish your power look as well. One way to carry both is to keep a slim purse with essentials such as lipstick, mirror, and money inside the attache case. If you need to go out to lunch, or any place where you choose not to carry the attache case, just pull out your purse and you're off.

Buying Quality Apparel

Aside from information on what articles of apparel to wear, a word on the quality of what you purchase is in order. Buy the best you can afford. If you are not gainfully employed, this may seem like impractical advice. But it still remains your best choice. Two really good suits with a variety of shirts or blouses will look better from the first day you own them than four suits of inferior quality—and will outlast them as well. To buy quality rather than quantity is a good habit to form.

> **Buy the best you can afford.**

Stretch your money by shopping sales or discount outlets if you wish. But remember, it isn't a bargain if it isn't right for you. A suit that never quite fits or isn't exactly your best shade is not a bargain no matter how many times it has been marked down.

In addition to buying natural fibers in clothing whenever possible, **invest in real leather** for shoes, attache case, and handbag—if you carry one. Leather conveys a professional look and will outlast the cheap looking imitations you might buy. In the end, we get what we pay for.

Your Arrival

You must arrive on time, preferably ten to fifteen minutes before the scheduled interview. Regardless of your reason, if you are late for the interview, it is almost impossible to recover from getting off to a poor start. If you are unfamiliar with the location of the interview, could have trouble finding parking, have a babysitter that has a habit of arriving late, or drive an undependable car—anything that could delay you—you must plan for the unpredictable. Scout the location the day prior to the interview or leave yourself extra time to get there on the day of the interview. Perhaps you should do both.

Always remember the importance of **the first five minutes** of the interview. You will be off to a very bad start if you miss your first five minutes altogether. You simply must find a way to arrive at the interview site ten to fifteen minutes prior to the stated interview time. This will give you time to compose yourself and check your appearance in a nearby restroom. If you expect to have application forms to fill out or security to clear, you should arrive even earlier.

However, if you arrive too early, kill some time by going for a cup of coffee or driving around the block. Try not to arrive at the office where you will be interviewed more than ten minutes early or you may make the receptionist and interviewer feel uncomfortable.

When you arrive at the office, introduce yourself to the receptionist and give the name of the person you are scheduled to see. The receptionist will probably ask you to be seated. Be courteous to this person as well as everyone you meet within the organization. Employers are known to solicit or consider the reactions of such employees toward interviewees prior to the final hiring decision.

If you wear a winter or rain coat to the interview, take it off in the outer office as soon as you arrive and leave it there during the interview.

While waiting in the outer office, be careful with the type of materials others may see you reading. Materials about the company are best because you may learn something about the company that you might comment on during the interview, and you will appear interested in the organization. If nothing is available on the company, your next choice should be a business magazine. Since you are already on display, make your choice of reading material a positive statement about you.

Overcoming Nervousness

While sitting in the outer office waiting to be called for the interview, you will probably feel nervous. This is human at a time like this. Instead of trying to rid yourself of these feelings, try to channel them productively. The same physiological process that makes you feel nervousness also makes you more alert than normal. It should keep you on your toes and help you respond better to questions during the interview.

You can better control your nervousness by following the same advice often given to public speakers. As you walk into the interview room, try to take slow deep breaths. You can do this subtly so the interviewer will be unaware of it. Although this is easier said than done, the more you can get your mind off yourself and concentrate on the other person, the more comfortable you will feel. If you are nervous, you are probably focusing too much attention on yourself. You are self-consciously concerned with how you are doing and what impression you are making on others. Try to be more other-directed. Rather than concentrate on your needs and fears, concern yourself with the employer's needs and questions.

Preparation is probably the greatest aid in lessening nervousness. If you have done your homework well—carried out the steps suggested in Chapter 7—you should walk into the interview feeling well prepared and confident. If you arrive early for the interview, you will have a chance to collect your thoughts, take those deep breaths, and focus your attention toward the employer.

Greeting the Interviewer

The receptionist may direct you to go meet with the interviewer or the interviewer may come out to meet you. Either way, stand to your full height before you take a step. Look alert, forceful, and energetic. If the interviewer comes out to meet you, walk over and shake his or her hand firmly.

If you are sent to the room where the interviewer is standing, walk toward him or her and shake hands. If he or she is seated and does not look up, stand up, or offer a handshake, you should wait a moment until the interviewer motions for you to be seated. If a lengthy time passes and the interviewer still does not acknowledge you, you may take a seat. However, wait for the interviewer to initiate the conversation.

9

Communicate Nonverbally

When you go into an interview, how will you communicate your competencies? On what basis will the interviewer determine if you are the right person for the job? Do you concentrate primarily on how you answer questions, or do you concern yourself with how you present yourself and convey your message? Will the interviewer make decisions based on your responses to questions or use some other criteria that have little to do with what you say? Whatever the case, you need to address these questions in the process of developing your interview strategy.

Consider some important research findings about how we communicate. Studies of the employment process, for example, show that 65-70% of a hiring decision may be based on nonverbal communication. This correlates closely with research findings in the field of nonverbal communication: approximately 65% of communication in most situations takes place through nonverbal channels. Moreover, if the verbal and nonverbal messages contradict one another, the nonverbal message is usually seen as more credible than the verbal one. The nonverbal message is viewed as more honest because it is the most difficult to control. Hence, the old saying that *"actions speak louder than words"* is a truism in the interview.

First Impressions

As noted in Chapter 8, interviewers admit that impressions formed during the first five minutes of the interview are seldom changed during the remainder of the interview. In at least 75% of the cases, the basic outcome of the interview has already been determined during those first few minutes!

If we ask, *"How can that be? How can anyone possibly make an important, objective, and informed decision in such a short period of time,"* the answer is, *"They probably can't."* Nonetheless, they often decide in this manner. Employers concentrate on nonverbal cues because very little verbal information—other than "small talk"—has been exchanged in the initial stages of the interview.

Being Likable

Remember, most people invited to an employment interview have already been "screened in." They supposedly possess the basic qualifications for the job, such as education and work experience. At this point employers will look for several qualities in the candidates, such as honesty, credibility, intelligence, competence, enthusiasm, spontaneity, friendliness, and likability. Much of the message communicating these qualities will be conveyed nonverbally.

In the end, employers hire people they **like** and who will interact well on an interpersonal basis with the rest of the staff. Therefore, you should communicate that you are a likable candidate who can get along well with others. You can communicate these messages by engaging in several nonverbal behaviors. Four of the most important ones include:

Important Nonverbal Behaviors

1. **Sit with a very slight forward lean toward the interviewer.** It should be so slight as to be almost imperceptible. If not overdone and obvious, it communicates your interest in what the interviewer is saying.

2. **Make eye contact frequently, but don't overdo it.** Good eye contact establishes better rapport with the interviewer. You will be perceived as more trustworthy if you will look at the interviewer as you ask and answer questions. To say someone has "shifty eyes" or cannot "look us in the eye" is to imply they may not be completely honest. To have a direct, though moderate eye gaze, conveys interest, and trustworthiness.

3. **A moderate amount of smiling will also help reinforce your positive image.** You should smile enough to convey your positive attitude, but not so much that you will not be taken seriously. Some people naturally smile often and others hardly ever smile. Monitor your behavior or ask a friend to give you honest feedback.

4. **Try to convey interest and enthusiasm through your vocal inflections.** Your tone of voice can say a lot about you and how interested you are in the interviewer and organization.

Communicating Class

A study reported by John Molloy in *Live For Success* indicated that 25 percent of personnel officers would not hire anyone with a wet hand-shake for an important position. If your hands tend to perspire when you are nervous, try using some talcum powder before leaving for the interview or wipe your hands on your handkerchief just before entering the outer office.

The way you stand, sit and walk—essentially how you carry yourself —has a bearing on how others perceive you. Molloy is convinced that the "look" that impresses interviewers the most is the upper middle class carriage—the look of class.

Even if your background is not upper middle class, as a youth you were probably told by someone in your family to improve how you stood, sat, and walked. Comments such as: *"Keep your shoulders back"* or *"Keep your head erect"* were good pieces of advice. If you did not pay much attention to them then, it would be to your advantage to do so now. The image of class includes these behaviors:

Image of Class

- Keep your shoulders back.
- Keep your head erect.
- Avoid folding your arms across your chest.
- Avoid sitting or standing with arms or legs far apart or what could be described as an "open" position.
- Use gestures that enhance your verbal message.

- Nod your head affirmatively at appropriate times—but do not overdo it.
- Project your voice loudly enough to be heard by the interviewer.
- Articulate clearly—do not mumble.
- Use pauses for emphasis.
- Watch your pace—avoid talking too fast or too slowly.
- Many people talk fast when they are nervous.
- Know yourself and regulate your pace accordingly.

Changing Your Behavior

Each of us has learned behaviors we reinforce daily. Many of these behaviors generate positive responses from others; but some of them are bad habits we should break. We can change our behaviors if we are strongly **motivated** to do so. But it is easy to slip back into the old patterns if we are not careful.

If you feel you need to break certain habits and learn new behaviors, you can make the changes. You must first be aware of the undesirable behavior you wish to replace as well as the desirable behavior you wish to acquire. Second, you must be aware of the undesirable behavior as it is taking place. For this you may need to enlist the aid of your spouse or good friend. Ask them to: *"Please observe me and inform me whenever I am doing _____."* After a while you will develop a greater awareness of the particular behavior as you are doing it.

Once conscious of our behavior, gradually we can become alert to the fact that we are about to engage in the behavior—early enough to alter the behavior. Given even more time of diligent awareness, the new behavior replaces the old one and eventually becomes as natural as the undesirable behavior once was.

Conducting effective interviews and getting a job that is right for you are significant reasons to motivate you to change some of your behaviors. If you think a behavior may be holding you back, try changing it now. The more time you give yourself, the more likely the change will become permanent and the less likely you will slip back into your former behavior in times of stress.

Listening

Listening is a learned skill. We learned to listen before we began our formal education—in fact, probably before we can even remember. Hence, we tend to believe listening is something we acquire automatically. While we can probably remember learning to play the piano, play baseball or to type, we usually can't recall learning to listen.

Being a good listener takes effort. You can't lean back in your chair and listen passively and listen well. Listening requires active involvement. Good listening will produce several important outcomes. You will have the information needed to help you ask better questions, respond to questions more effectively, and eventually to make a decision as to whether this is a job that is really fit for you. In order to do this, you should:

Good Listening Behaviors

1. **Focus your attention on the interviewer and what he or she is saying.** Don't let your mind wander to such things as: the strange or good looking appearance of the interviewer; the photographs on the desk; your fears about not getting the job offer; or your plans for that evening or the weekend. We can listen and comprehend information about four times faster than the speaker can talk. Don't use that extra time to let your mind wander, but rather to concentrate on the other person's message.

2. **Look beyond the personal appearance or mannerisms of the interviewer or any irritating words or ideas as you listen for content.** Don't let certain annoying words, ideas or mannerisms of the interviewer so prejudice you that you can't listen objectively to what is being said.

3. **Try to listen for information and withhold evaluation of the message until later.** This may be difficult to do, but it makes an important difference in what you get from the message. As we evaluate, our thoughts are on our reaction to the message, and thus we miss part of what the other person is saying.

4. Give positive nonverbal feedback to the interviewer. Nod in agreement occasionally if you agree, and smile occasionally if appropriate. Most everyone likes to receive positive responses from others. Since most people interpret no response as a negative response, avoid an expressionless face. Your feedback is also likely to be interpreted as a sign of interest on your part.

If you try to concentrate on what is being said rather than how you are doing, you will most likely create a good impression on the interviewer. Being other-directed with your nonverbal communication will make you seem more likable and competent than many other candidates who remain self concerned and nervous throughout the interview.

10

Manage the Verbal Interchange

W hile nonverbal communication is extremely important in the interview, so too is the verbal interchange. Employers want to hear you talk about yourself and the job. They are concerned with both what you say and how you say it. Therefore, your verbal communication should reinforce the positive image you are communicating nonverbally.

Employer's Needs

Put yourself in the position of the interviewer for a few moments. You invited a candidate to an interview based upon his or her cover letter, resume, application form, and perhaps a telephone screening interview. Within a short period of time—a 30 to 60 minute interview—you must now fully assess the interviewee's attitudes, motivations, behaviors, and skills. You want to know what this person can and will do for you. Making a mistake can cost you a great deal of time and money. Studies show companies spend thousands of dollars hiring individuals. The initial costs include announcing the vacancy, screening resumes and letters, interviewing candidates, and settling on a salary/benefit package. The long-term hiring expenses include training costs and the possibility of repeating the whole hiring process—which may include unemployment compensation and/or severance pay, if the individual must be terminated or resigns. Regardless of how hard you try, you can still make mistakes hiring what appeared to be the best candidate. As many interviewers have learned after years of interviewing experience, assessment techniques are at best only rough indicators of performance.

From the employer's perspective, hiring is a risky and expensive business. He or she wants someone who can do the job well—someone worth the salary and benefits. The employer also wants someone who will be a good representative to others outside the organization. The person should be able to get along well with supervisors and co-workers inside the organization. Translating these concerns into questions, most interviewers want to know:

> **From the employer's perspective, hiring is a risky and expensive business.**

- Why should I hire you?

- What kind of person are you?

- Why are you looking for a job? Why here?

- What kind of employee will you make in our organization— willingness to take responsibility as well as directions, be productive, loyal, creative, entrepreneurial, enthusiastic?

- Do you have a demonstrated and sustained interest in this work?

- What motivates you?

- Do your credentials demonstrate that you are a purposeful individual who gets things done?

- How much will you cost us?

- What haven't you told us about yourself?

- What are your weaknesses?

- Will you be able to work with your supervisors and other employees in this organization?

- Why do you want to leave your present employer?

- How long will you stay with us before you start looking for another job?

While most interviewers will not bluntly ask you all these questions, they will seek answers by asking other questions which may give them cues to your behavior.

The Competent Interviewer

Interviewers also are concerned about conducting effective interviews. Like interviewees, interviewers vary in quality. Some interviewers are well trained and experienced in the art of interviewing. They know how to put the interviewee at ease and draw out the information needed for the final assessment. Other interviewers are less successful. Some may be in training or have little experience. Still others may be incompetent or in need of major re-training. Expect to encounter all types.

If you find yourself with a well trained and experienced interviewer, you can expect him or her to conduct the interview in a professional manner and according to a particular pattern. Most trained interviewers are versed in six rules for conducting effective interviews:

1. The interviewer will be sensitive to the candidate, respect his or her intelligence, and not act superior.

2. The interviewer will try to put the candidate at ease rather than create stress.

3. Following the initial "icebreakers" the interviewer will state the objective of the interview.

4. The interviewer will try to get the candidate to talk as much as possible without drilling him or her with questions.

5. The interviewer will seek valid information and not interject personal opinions into the interview. He or she will be professional at all times.

6. The interviewer will know when and how to close the interview. This includes clearly summarizing the candidate's interview statements so there will be no misunderstandings about what was communicated.

In well managed interviews, you will be expected to talk a great deal about yourself and the job. The interviewer will especially want to know about your goals and your value to him or her.

Most interviewers are competent people trying their best to do a good job. However, well trained and prepared interviewers are the exception rather than the rule. You most frequently will be interviewed by someone who has previous experience interviewing. Whether they are professionally trained is another question. Some interviewers will ask irrelevant, illegal, or stressful questions, or they may have difficulty formulating and asking enough questions to keep the interview flowing. Some questions may be redundant; you already answered them on your resume or employment application. If you encounter irrelevant, illegal, or stressful questions, try to be tactful. In the case of the inept interviewer, you may feel you are not being given a chance to put your best foot forward. Be prepared to take some initiative in this interview by asking questions which will indicate your strengths and value to the interviewer. If the interviewer's questions seem too broad or vague, try to refocus or narrow them. You might do this by asking a question, *"By _____ do you mean _____?"*

The Interview Sequence

While interviewers do not follow an exact pattern of questioning, most of them do follow a basic sequence which you should be aware of and manage to your advantage. The sequence will approximate this:

1. Greeting

2. Establishing common ground/icebreakers

3. Indicating purpose of interview

4. Drawing out information through the exchange of questions and answers:

- General and specific questions
- Brief and drawn out answers
- Conversations to clarify questions, explain answers, and reach mutual understanding

5. Summarizing information and understanding

6. Indicating next steps to be taken

7. Closing

The greeting will be short—probably some variation of *"How do you do Miss Smith. I am John Jones. Glad you could come in this morning."* Following the greeting, but before going into the reason for the interview, you will engage in a few minutes of small talk. This is a chance for both of you to feel more at ease. If you know something about the interviewer's interests—either from information gathered in your research or because of something you see in the office—you might use this topic to establish common ground.

> **Avoid negatives by presenting yourself in as positive light as possible.**

Small talk for establishing common ground is important. For example, we know a young woman who applied for a teaching position at a community college. A few weeks earlier, she had read Mager's book on behavioral objectives for instruction. At the beginning of the interview, she noticed a copy of Mager's book lying on the interviewer's desk and commented about it. The interviewer was pleased to learn she was familiar with Mager's work, and indicated none of the other applicants were familiar with it. She is convinced to this day that it was a major factor in getting the job offer. It established common ground and set her apart from the many other people applying for the same position.

The interviewer may next talk about the purpose of the interview as he or she attempts to "get down to business." The company or the specific position will become the major subject. At this point, the interviewer may be very persuasive, even attempting to "sell" the applicant on the position. Most of the interview time will be spent on the "drawing out information" phase—which is the primary focus of the remainder of this chapter. Salary negotiations, which may or may not take place at the initial interview, are discussed in Chapter 11. The close of the interview will be dealt with in Chapter 12.

Use Positive Form

The way you phrase your questions and answers can be as important as the actual content of your communication. What you want to achieve is **positive form.** This means avoiding negatives by presenting yourself in as positive a light as possible. In the interview, several opportunities arise for enhancing your image through the use of positive form.

The first use of positive form relates to **names.** Each of us likes to be called by our name. Make sure you get the name of the interviewer, get it right, and use it from time to time as you speak. Use the interviewer's title (Miss, Mrs., Mr., Dr., Professor, etc.) and last name. Never call the interviewer by his or her first name unless specifically requested to do so—even if the interviewer uses your first name. Many interviewers will be offended by such familiarity.

A second use of positive form is inherent in the **way you phrase questions and answers.** For example, rather than ask *"What are the duties of _____ position?"*, ask *"What would be my duties?"* This form of questioning subtly plants the positive thought of you in the position. This is not presumptuous because you use the word *"would,"* which indicates you are not overly sure of yourself.

A third use of positive form relates to **good grammar.** Proper use of language is not something to be left in the English classroom. Many so-called "educated" people do not use good grammar, and many of these people do not interview successfully. Check your use of grammar. If it is not impeccable, make an effort to improve it before the interview.

Fourth, use **good diction.** One of the most common problems is to shorten words. How many people do you hear say *"goin"* instead of *"going,"* or *"gonna"* rather then *"going to"*? Another problem is substituting, eliminating, or adding consonants: *"Adlanta"* rather than *"Atlanta," "din't"* rather than *"didn't," "idear"* rather than *"idea."* Do you do this? Do you ever say *"yea"* rather than *"yes"*? The use of sloppy speech is a habit many people—including the well educated—get into. But it is a habit—a learned and reinforced behavior—you can change. If you have a tendency to modify words these in manners, it is a habit worth correcting.

Fifth, avoid using **vocalized pauses.** An occasional silence is acceptable and preferable to overuse of *"ahs"* and *"uhms."* Try not to fill silences with *"ah"* or *"and ah."* Vocalized pauses distract the listener from your message and the excessive use can be annoying.

Sixth, avoid the use of **fillers.** Fillers add no information and, if overdone, also distract the listener. The most commonly used fillers are *"you know," "like"* and *"okay."* If used frequently, the listener becomes distracted and will find it hard to concentrate on the content of your message.

Seventh, use **active verbs**. When talking about what you have done or will do, active verbs like *"organized," "analyzed,"* or *"supervised"* are preferable to the nouns *"organizer," "analyst,"* or *"supervisor."* Even stronger action words can be used to indicate your present strengths: *"organize," "analyze,"* and *"supervise."* Avoid the passive voice. For example, instead of saying *"The entire conference was organized by me"* (passive), say *"I organized the entire conference"* (active).

Eighth, avoid using **tentative, indecisive terms**, such as *"I think," "I guess," "I feel."* If you use them excessively, they will negatively affect the impression you are trying to leave with the interviewer. Research indicates that women use these tentative terms more frequently than men. By using these indecisive terms, you can—male or female—appear indecisive and somewhat muddled. You want to communicate that you are a clear and purposeful individual.

> **Present your strengths— skills and accomplishments —in a positive way.**

Ninth, avoid the use of ambiguous and somewhat **negative terms** such as *"pretty good"* or *"fairly well."* These terms say little if anything. They may even communicate negatives—that what you did was not good!

Most people could improve their use of positive form. But it is difficult for someone to follow those suggestions after reading them the night before the interview. One needs to begin making the necessary changes well in advance of the interview. It can be done if one really wants to make the changes, but for most people it takes concerted effort over time. Follow the advice for changing behaviors in Chapter 9 so these changes will become your natural behaviors. By all means, do not pass up the nine opportunities for using positive form in the interview.

Analyze Your Listener and Use Supports

Public speakers are always advised to analyze both their audience and their situation before speaking. The same advice should be followed when you interview. **The language you use should vary according to the interviewer.** If the interviewer is from the personnel office with little or no background in your field of expertise, your language should be less technical than it would be if you were talking with someone who shares your technical background. If you are interviewing with someone in your area of expertise, who also has the technical background, you should use a vocabulary relevant to the job in order to build common ground as well as your credibility. But don't overdo the use of jargon.

Analysis of your situation should tell you this is not the time for excessive modesty. Of course, you do not want to become an obnoxious braggart, but you do want to present your strengths—skills and accomplishments—in a positive way. Therefore, don't be reluctant to **talk about yourself and your accomplishments**. Remember, the interviewer wants to know more about you, especially your potential value to him or her. The more positive information you can communicate to the interviewer, the stronger your position will be in the final hiring decision.

When you make statements about your skills or accomplishments, try to back them up with **supports**. Can you give an **example** of how you improved production on your last job? Can you **describe** the sales campaign that won you the Best-Copywriter-of-the-Year Award? Can you **compare** the previous bookkeeping system with the one you instituted that saved your last employer so much money? Can you cite **figures** that demonstrate how you increased sales at the last company you worked for?

When you back up your assertions with supports, you gain several advantages over individuals who do not. Supports help clarify your comments; help substantiate them; help the listener recall them at a later time; and they add interest. Supports include such things as:

- examples
- illustrations
- descriptions
- definitions

- statistics
- comparisons
- testimonials

Use such supports to emphasize your accomplishments.

A frequent question asked by prospective interviewers is *"How honest should I be?"* Most individuals have something in their background they believe would work against them in getting the job if the interviewer knew about it. They wonder if they should tell the interviewer before he or she finds out. We advise you to be honest—but not stupid. In other words, if asked a direct question about the thing you hoped to hide, answer honestly, but emphasize positives. Under no circumstances should you volunteer your negatives or weaknesses. The next section will show you some ways to manage questions about your weaknesses.

Manage Questions With Positive Content

The actual content of your answers should be stated in the positive. One example of this is the type of hobbies you communicate to employers. As John Molloy notes, many employers prefer "active" hobbies, such as swimming, tennis, golfing, or jogging, to more sedentary activities, such as reading and stamp collecting.

But the most important examples of positive content relate to managing the specific interview questions which are designed to probe your knowledge, abilities, motivations, strengths, and weaknesses. The employer's goal is somewhat negative in the interview; he or she wants to know why **not** to hire you. The major unstated question is *"What are your weaknesses?"* Several other questions may be asked to indirectly answer this major one.

You should always phrase your answers to questions in a positive manner. Avoid the use of such commonly used negatives as *"can't,"* *"didn't,"* and *"wouldn't."* These terms direct listeners into negative avenues of thinking. They do not communicate optimism and enthusiasm—two qualities you should demonstrate in the interview. Take, for example, two different answers to the following interview question.

QUESTION: *Why did you major in business administration?*

ANSWER 1:   *That's real funny. I wanted to major in history, but my parents told me if they were footing the bills, I shouldn't be studying useless subjects. I tried political science, biology, and accounting*

*but didn't like any of them. Business adminis-
tration wasn't that difficult for me. I couldn't
think of anything I like more—except perhaps
history. And it's not a bad field to be in these
days.*

ANSWER 2: *I always enjoyed business and wanted to make
it a career. As a youth I had my own paper
route, sold books door to door, and was a
member of Junior Achievement. In college I was
involved in a couple of small businesses. It
seems as though I have always been in business.
I tend to have a knack for it, and I love it. My
major in business administration further streng-
thened my desire to go into business. It gave me
better direction. What I want is to work with a
small and growing firm that would use my
abilities to plan and implement marketing
strategies.*

While the first answer may be the most truthful, it presents a negative and
haphazard image of you. The second answer, while also truthful, stresses
the positive by communicating strengths, purpose, and enthusiasm.

Let's take as another example an employer who asks the interviewee
why he is leaving his present job:

QUESTION: *Why do you want to leave your present job?*

ANSWER 1: *After working there three years, I don't feel I
am going anywhere. Morale isn't very good,
and the management doesn't reward us according to our productivity. I really don't like working there anymore.*

ANSWER 2: *After working there three years, I have learned
a great deal about managing people and developing new markets. But it is time for me to
move on to a larger and more progressive
organization where I can use my marketing
experience in several different areas. I am ready*

to take on more responsibilities. This change will be a positive step in my professional growth.

Again, the first answer communicates too many negatives. The second answer is positive and upbeat in its orientation toward skills, accomplishments, and the future.

Most interview questions can be answered by using positive language that further emphasizes that you are competent, intelligent, friendly, spontaneous, honest, and likable. This language should project your strengths, purpose, and enthusiasm. If you feel you need to practice formulating positive responses to interview questions, examine the sample questions outlined in Chapter 7. Consider alternative positive responses to each question. You also may want your spouse or friend to ask you questions. Tape record the interview and review your responses. Are your answers positive in both form and content? Do they communicate your strengths, purpose, and enthusiasm? Keep practicing the interview until you automatically respond with positive yet truthful answers.

Overcome Objections and Negatives

Interviewers are likely to have certain objections to hiring you. Some of their objections may be legitimate whereas others are misunderstandings. Objections might relate to any of the illegal questions outlined in Chapter 7—marital status, sex, or age. But many objections are perfectly legal and are common ways of discriminating one candidate from another. Among these objections are questions relating to your bona fide qualifications—education, experience, and skills.

If you are weak in any of the qualification areas, you may not be able to overcome the objections unless you acquire the necessary qualifications. But chances are these qualifications have been screened prior to the interview and thus will not be a topic of discussion. If, on the other hand, your education, experience, and skill level pose any objections in the mind of the interviewer, stress again your strengths in a positive and enthusiastic manner. Objections to your educational background will be the easiest to deal with if your experience and skills demonstrate your value.

On the other hand, one objection individuals increasingly encounter today from employers is being **over-qualified**. More and more people by choice are moving **down** in their careers rather than up. Given the desire for and ease of higher education, more and more people appear over-educated for many jobs today.

Employers' objections to candidates being over-qualified are a legitimate concern. From the perspective of employers, the over-qualified individual may quickly become a liability. Becoming unhappy with the job, they leave after a short period of time. Other individuals may have an unrealistic ambition of quickly moving up the organizational ladder. In either case, the over-qualified individual may cost an employer more than he or she is worth.

On the other hand, the over-qualified candidate may think he or she is doing the employer a favor—the company is getting more for their money. If this is your perception of your value, you need to change it immediately. Unless you are prepared to take a position which is beneath your qualifications and can clearly communicate your desire to the employer so as to lessen his or her fears, you will most likely not get the job. In the interview you must convince the employer that you understand his or her apprehension about you, but you are willing, able, and eager to do the job.

While you want to communicate your strengths, employers want to know your weaknesses. There are several ways to handle questions that try to get at your weaknesses. If the interviewer frankly asks you *"What are some of your weaknesses?"*, be prepared to give him or her positive responses. You can do this in any of five different ways:

1. **Discuss a negative which is not related to the job being considered:**

   I don't enjoy accounting. I know it's important, but I find it boring. Even at home my wife takes care of our books. Marketing is what I like to do. Other people are better at bookkeeping than I am. I'm glad this job doesn't involve accounting!

2. **Discuss a "negative" which can also be a positive:**

   I'm somewhat of a workaholic. I love my work, but I sometimes don't spend enough time with my family. I've been going into the office seven days a week, and I often put in 12 hour days. I'm now learning to better manage my time. I've created better balance in my life and with my family.

3. Discuss a negative which the interviewer already knows:

I spent a great deal of time working on advanced degrees, as indicated in my resume, and thus I lack extensive work experience. However, I believe my education has prepared me well for this job. My leadership experience in college taught me how to work with people, organize, and solve problems. I write well and quickly. My research experience helped me analyze, synthesize, and develop strategies.

4. Discuss a negative which you have improved upon:

I used to get over-committed and miss important deadlines. But then I read a book on time management and learned what I was doing wrong. Within three weeks I reorganized my use of time and found I could meet my deadlines with little difficulty. The quality of my work also improved. Now I have time to work out at the gym each day. I'm doing more and feeling better at the same time.

Part of the analysis of your audience—the interviewer—may include determining what concerns the employer may have about you, but may not ask. For example, if you are retired and decide to pursue a second career, you may expect some employers to be hesitant to hire you. Some of their concerns might include your health: would you be out a lot because of illness; your ability to fit into a new work environment: would it be difficult for you to take direction from someone younger than yourself—especially if you had been a senior level manager in your pre-retirement position. Anticipate concerns you believe the interviewer may have but be reluctant to raise. It may be to your advantage to raise them—especially if you are able to put a positive spin on the situation.

Handle Silence Positively

Many people feel uncomfortable with silence and treat silence as if it were an enemy. It can be your worst enemy if your response is to fill the silence and you begin rambling on about anything in order to fill the space.

Be careful of silence. There may be a pause because the interviewer is considering a remark you just made or is deciding what to question next. The pause may be intentional on the part of the interviewer to see how you will handle yourself. Will you be comfortable with the silence or will you try to fill it with whatever comes to mind? You have two choices that are positive ones for your candidacy. You may keep silent and wait for the interviewer to continue or you might ask the interviewer if he would like to know more about _____. Of course _____ is an area of strength that you welcome an opportunity to talk about. If you choose the second option, keep your comments focused and relatively short.

Take Initiative

Employment recruiters on college campuses indicate that the most appealing candidates are those who take some initiative during the interview. We are not suggesting that you take control of the interview, but you need not play a completely passive role either. Taking initiative is a quality many employers prize in their employees. Indeed, many employers wish they could find more employees who would take initiative.

Even with the best interviewer, you will need to ask questions. Remember, you have a decision to make too. Are you really interested in the job? Does it fit your goals and skills? Will it give you the chance to do something you do well and enjoy doing? Will it give you an opportunity to move in some of the directions you want to move? Use the interview situation to get answers to these and other questions that are critical to your future.

Ask questions that help sell your skills. Ask questions that clarify the scope of the position and will help you determine whether this job is right for you. Do not ask questions that should have been answered by your basic research on the company, and do not ask questions about job benefits until after you are actually offered the job.

11

Negotiate Salary

W hat are you really worth in today's job market? How much should you be paid in dollars? Can you demonstrate your value to employers? What dollar value will the employer assign to you? What salary are you willing to accept?

You think you are worth a lot. After impressing upon the employer that you are the right person for the job, the bottom line becomes money—your labor in exchange for the employer's cash and benefits. How, then, are you going to deal with these questions in order to get more than the employer may initially be willing to offer?

Demonstrate Your Value

The salary question is awkward for many applicants who are reluctant to talk about money. They think one must take what is offered because salaries are set by employers. Such thinking is unfortunate, because it means many people are paid less than what they could be getting if they knew some basic techniques for negotiating salaries. Most people are probably underpaid by $3,000 because they don't use such techniques.

Except for many entry-level positions for people without experience, salary is seldom predetermined. Most employers have some flexibility to **negotiate** salary. While they do not try to exploit applicants, neither do they want to pay applicants more than what they are willing to accept.

Salaries are usually assigned to positions or jobs rather than to individuals. But not everyone is of equal value in performing the job;

some are more productive than others. Since individual performance differs, you should attempt to establish **your** value in the eyes of the employer rather than accept a salary figure for the job. The art of salary negotiation will help you do this.

Money In Your Future

We all have financial needs which our salary helps to meet. But salary has other significance too. It is an indicator of our worth to others. It also influences our future income. Therefore, it should be treated as one of the most serious considerations in the job interview. The salary you receive today will influence your future earnings. Yearly salary increments will be figured as a percentage of your base salary. When changing jobs, expect employers to offer you a salary similar to the one you earned in your last job. Once they learn what you made in your previous job, they will probably offer you a salary that at best represents a ten to fifteen percent increase over your previous salary, regardless of your current or projected productivity. If you hope to improve your income in the long run, then you must be willing to negotiate your salary from a position of strength.

> **Establish your value in the eyes of the employer rather than accept a salary figure for the job.**

Prepare For the Money Questions

You should be well prepared to deal with the question of salary anytime during your job search but especially during the job interview. Based on your library research on salary ranges for different positions (Chapter 4) as well as salary information gained from your networking activities (Chapter 6), you should know the approximate salary range for the position you are seeking. If you fail to gather this salary information prior to the screening or job interview, you may do yourself a disservice by accepting too low a figure or pricing yourself out of consideration. It is always best to be informed so you can be in better control to negotiate salary and benefits.

Raise the Financial Question

The question of salary may be raised anytime during the job search. Employers may want you to state a salary expectation figure on an application form, in a cover letter, or over the telephone. Most frequently, however, employers will talk about salary during the employment interview. If at all possible, keep the salary question open until the very last. Even with application forms, cover letters, and telephone screening interviews, try to delay the discussion of salary by stating "open" or "negotiable." After all, the ultimate purpose of your job search activities is to **demonstrate your value to employers**. You should not attempt to translate your value into dollar figures until you have had a chance to convince the employer of your worth. This is best done near the end of the job interview.

> **Keep the salary question open until the very last.**

Employers traditionally assign salary to the job or position rather than the individual. Although they will have a salary figure or range in mind when they interview you, they still want to know your salary expectations. How much will you cost them? Will it be more or less than the job is worth? Employers preferably want to hire individuals for the least amount possible. You, on the other hand, want to be hired for as much as possible. Obviously, there is room for disagreement and unhappiness as well as negotiation and compromise.

One easy way employers screen you in or out of consideration is to raise the salary question early in the interview. A standard question is *"What are your salary requirements?"* When asked, avoid answering with a specific dollar figure. You should aim at establishing your **value** in the eyes of the employer prior to talking about a figure. If you give the employer a salary figure at this stage, you are likely to lock yourself into it, regardless of how much you impress the employer or what you find out about the duties of the job. Therefore, salary should be the last major item you discuss with the employer.

You should never ask about salary prior to being offered the job, even though it is one of your major concerns. Try to let the employer initiate the salary question. And when he or she does, take your time. Don't appear too anxious. While you may know—based on your previous research—approximately what the employer will offer, try to get the employer to state a figure first. If you do this, you will be in a stronger negotiating position.

When the salary question arises, assuming you cannot or do not want to put it off until later, your first step should be to clearly summarize the job responsibilities/duties as you understand them. At this point you are attempting to do two things:

1. Seek clarification from the interviewer as to the actual job and all it involves.

2. Emphasize the level of skills required in the most positive way. In other words, you emphasize the value and worth of this position to the organization and subtly this may help support the actual salary figure that the interviewer or you later provide.

You might do this, for example, by saying,

As I understand it, I would report directly to the vice-president in charge of marketing and I would have full authority for marketing decisions that involved expenditures of up to $50,000. I would have a staff of five people—a secretary, two copywriters, and two marketing assistants.

Such a summary statement establishes for both you and the interviewer that (1) this position reports to the highest levels of authority; (2) this position is responsible for decision-making involving fairly large sums of money; and (3) this position involves supervision of staff.

Although you may not explicitly draw the connection, you are emphasizing the value of this position to the organization. This position should be worth a lot more than one in which the hiree will report to the marketing manager, be required to get approval for all expenditures over $100, and has no staff—just access to the secretarial pool! By doing this you will focus the salary question (that you have not yet responded to) around the exact work you must perform on the job in exchange for salary and benefits. You have also seized the opportunity to focus on the value of the person who will be selected to fill this vacancy.

Your conversation might go something like this. The employer poses the question:

What are your salary requirements?

Your first response should be to summarize the responsibilities of the position:

> *Let me see if I understand all that is involved with this position and job. I would be expected to _____. Have I covered everything or are there some other responsibilities I should know about?*

This response focuses the salary question around the value of the position in relation to you. After the interviewer responds to your final question, answer the initial salary question in this manner:

> *What is the normal range in your company for a position such as this?*

This question establishes the value as well as the range for the **position or job**—two important pieces of information you need before proceeding further into the salary negotiation stage. The employer normally will give you the requested salary range. Once he or she does, depending on how you feel about the figure, you can follow up with one more question:

> *What would be the normal salary range for someone with my qualifications?*

This question further attempts to establish the value for the **individual** versus the position. This line of questioning attempts to yield the salary expectations of the employer without revealing your desired salary figure or range. It also should indicate whether the employer distinguishes between individuals and positions when establishing salary figures.

Reach Agreement

After finding out what the employer is prepared to offer, you have several choices. First, you can indicate that the figure is acceptable to you and thus conclude your final interview. Second, you can haggle for more money in the hope of reaching an acceptable compromise. Third, you can delay final action by asking for more time to consider the offer. Finally, you can tell the employer the figure is unacceptable and leave.

The first and the last options may indicate you are either too eager or playing hard-to-get. We recommend the second and third options. If you decide to reach agreement on salary in this interview, haggle in a professional manner. You can do this best by establishing a salary range from which to bargain in relation to the employer's salary range. For example, if the employer indicates that he or she is prepared to offer $40,000 to $45,000, and these figures are consistent with the salary data you gathered in your informational interviews, you should establish common ground for negotiation by placing your salary range into the employer's range. Your response to the employer's $40,000 to $45,000 range might be:

> *Yes, that does come near what I was expecting. My expectations are between $43,000 and $48,000.*

You, in effect, **place the top of the employer's range into the bottom of your range**. At this point you should be able to negotiate a salary of $45,000 to $47,000, depending on how much flexibility the employer has with salaries. Most employers have more flexibility than they are willing to admit.

Once you have placed your expectations at the top of the employer's salary range, you need to emphasize your value. Remember the supports we discussed in Chapter 10. It is not enough to simply state you were "thinking" in a certain range; you must state **why** you believe you are worth what you want. You might say, for example,

> *The salary surveys I've read indicate that the salary for the position of _____ in this industry and region is between $43,000 and $48,000. Since, as we have discussed, I have extensive experience in all the areas you outlined, I would not need training in the job duties themselves—just a brief orientation to the operating procedures you use here at _____. I'm sure I could be up and running in this job within a week or two. Taking everything in consideration—especially my skills and experience and what I see as my future contributions here—I really feel a salary of $48,000 is fair compensation. Is this possible here at _____?*

Another option is to ask the employer for time to think about the salary offer. Ask to sleep on it for a day or two. A common professional courtesy is to give you at least 48 hours to consider an offer. During this time, you may want to carefully examine the job. Is it worth what you are being offered? Can you do better? What are other employers offering for comparable positions? If one or two other employers are considering you for a job, let this employer know his or her job is not the only one under consideration. Let the employer know you may be in demand elsewhere. This should give you a better bargaining position. Contact the other employers and let them know you have a job offer and that you would

> **Negotiate from a position of strength—not greed.**

like to have your application status with them clarified before you make any decisions with the other employer. Depending on how much flexibility an employer may have to accelerate a hiring decision, you may be able to go back to the first employer with another job offer. With a second job offer in hand, you may greatly enhance your bargaining position.

In both recommended options, you need to keep in mind that you should negotiate from a position of strength—not greed. Establish your value, learn what the employer is willing to pay, and negotiate in a professional manner. How you handle the salary negotiations will affect your future relations with the employer. In general, applicants who negotiate well will be treated well on the job.

Take Benefits

Many employers will try to impress candidates with the benefits offered by the company. These might include retirement, bonuses, stock options, medical and life insurance, and cost of living adjustments. If the employer includes these benefits in the salary negotiations, do not be overly impressed. Most benefits are standard—they come with the job. When negotiating salary, it is best to talk about specific dollar figures.

On the other hand, if the salary offered by the employer does not meet your expectations, but you still want the job, you might try to negotiate for some benefits which are not considered standard. These might include longer paid vacations, some flextime, and profit sharing.

Renegotiate the Future

In some cases you may want a job even though it does not meet your immediate salary expectations. The employer may not be able to add special benefits to satisfy you. When this happens, you might request during the interview that the employer reconsider your salary after six months on the job. Another approach is to ask the employer to consider expanding the job description or upgrading the position and salary. Such provisions would give you time to demonstrate your value. Employers have little to lose and much to gain by agreeing to such a provision. If other negotiating approaches fail, this one is at least worth trying.

Don't Expect Too Much

Many applicants have unrealistic salary expectations and exaggerated notions of their worth to potential employers. In recent years several unions began renegotiating contracts in a new direction—downwards. Unions gave back salary increases and benefits won in previous years in order to maintain job security in the face of deepening recessions. Workers in many industries were not in a position to further increase their salaries. Many employers believed salaries had become extremely inflated in relation to profits. Such salaries, in turn, created even more inflated salary expectations among job hunters.

Given the declining power of unions, turbulent economic conditions, the increased prevalence of "give-back" schemes, and greater emphasis on productivity and performance in the workplace, many employers are reluctant to negotiate salaries upwards prior to seeing the hiree perform in their organization. Others rely on company bonuses or other forms of compensation to reward top performers. In tight job market situations, many employers feel they can maintain their ground on salary offers. After all, as more well qualified candidates glut the job market, many are willing to take lower salaries.

Given this situation, you may find it increasingly difficult to negotiate better salaries with employers. You will need to stress your value more than ever. For example, if you think you are worth $50,000, will you be productive enough to generate $300,000 of business for the company to justify that amount? If you can't translate your salary expectations into dollars and cents profits for the employer, perhaps you should not be negotiating at all!

12

Close, Follow-Up and Implement

Y ou need to take the initiative to keep in contact with the employer during his or her final deliberations. This can be done by closing the interview in a particular manner.

The end of the interview is often an awkward time for both the interviewee and the interviewer. You are worried about the overall impression you have made on the employer. You may feel you forgot to communicate important information about your strengths. But the time has come to finish the interview.

Close the Interview

At the close of nearly every interview, the interviewer verbalizes some variation of, *"Glad you could come by today. We have several other people to interview. We'll be in touch."* In response, most interviewees shake hands, thank the interviewer, and leave. Don't do this!

At this point, try to **briefly** summarize your strengths as they relate to the job. For example,

I'm really glad I had the chance to talk with you. I know with what I learned when I reorganized the accounting department at XYZ Corporation, I could increase your profits too.

In addition, ask the interviewer when he or she expects to make the hiring decision. If the response is *"Friday of next week,"* then ask, *"If I haven't heard by Monday, may I give you a call?"* Almost everyone will say you may, and you will have solved your problem of wondering when you will hear about the final decision and what to do next. If you haven't heard anything by the time the designated Monday arrives, do call. Some interviewers use this technique to see if you will follow through with a call—others are just inconsiderate.

Respond to a Job Offer

Occasionally the interviewee will be offered the job right on the spot. This may happen if you have made a particularly good impression, if it is a hard position to fill, or if the employer needs to fill it fast. Even if you think you want the position, it is a good idea to ask for a period of time—at least a day or two—to consider the offer. There are several reasons why you should do this. First, give yourself time to weigh the advantages and disadvantages of the position. It is possible that a job which seems good, as described by the interviewer, may seem less so after you've had a chance to think about it. This advice is doubly important if you have been sent to the interview through any employment agency. In this case, if you accept and later turn down the position, you may be liable for the fee. If it is a "fee paid" position—paid by the employer—you are still likely to be held responsible for paying the fee if you accept but never actually go to work or work less than a specified period of time—often six months to a year. These regulations vary by state as well as employment agency, but be especially careful about accepting a job you are uncertain about.

A second reason to ask for time to think about the job offer is to give yourself a chance to check with other prospective employers who are considering you for employment. It is usually acceptable to call a firm where you have been told you are under consideration and tell them you have a job offer. It may speed up their decision and give you two offers from which to compare, bargain, and choose.

Third, as noted in the previous chapter, asking for time to consider the offer can give you greater leverage for negotiating salary. You will be further communicating your value to the employer.

Send Thank You Letters

Always follow up the interview by sending a thank you letter. Do this within 24 hours after the interview. It is a thoughtful, courteous thing to do and will often set you apart from the other applicants who normally do not do this. Examples of thank you letters are found in Appendix B.

If you send the thank you letter right away, it may arrive while the hiring deliberations are in progress. In addition to expressing your gratitude for the interview, briefly restate the reasons you believe you are right for the job. Again, stress your value—what you will do for the employer.

Even if you are not hired, send a thank you letter and ask to be remembered for future openings. Based on the thoughtfulness of your thank you letter, you might be hired for an even better job in the future.

> **Always follow up the interview by sending a thank you letter.**

Continue the Process

If you do not receive a job offer or if you decide the job is not for you, continue conducting informational interviews, networking, and checking on other job leads. You may go through interviews with several organizations before you find the job you really want. In your personal contacts as well as any thank you letters you write after rejecting a job offer or in response to a rejection, **ask to be remembered and referred**. There are other jobs out there.

Once you accept a job offer, send letters to the people who helped you with your job search. Inform them of your decision and thank them for their assistance. You should keep in contact periodically with people in your networks. Remember, you will probably make several other job or career changes in the future. These people are important sources for job information. They may give you leads to better opportunities three, five, or ten years from now. While you may not make frequent job changes, you never know what can happen. It is best to keep your networks up-to-date for both personal and professional reasons.

Succeed Through Implementation

So where are you now? Let's hope you are out making contacts, conducting informational interviews, and interviewing on a regular basis. You cannot just read a book and hope something will happen to you.

The key to job search success in getting interviews and job offers is **implementation**. You must take the job search techniques and translate them into specific action plans. This involves setting daily and weekly job search goals and specifying activities you will regularly engage in. For example, your goal for three weeks from now may be to get one job interview. In order to achieve this goal, plan to send out three resumes each day in response to job listings, make five telephone calls each day for uncovering job leads, and conduct three informational interviews each day. In other words, plan to devote a large amount of time to your job search in order to get the results you want.

If you do not plan and spend time in this manner, do not expect to get ahead in your job search. At best, you will have purchased this book and spent some time reading it. The book is only good if you develop an action plan for making it work for you. The same is true for the other career planning books discussed in Appendix C.

The hardest job you may ever do is finding a job. Hard work, persistence, drive, and intelligent action planning will put you in the right places to seize job opportunities that are right for you. We wish you well and hope you enthusiastically and diligently **implement** your job search in order to get those interviews and job offers which can make an important difference in your life. If you do this, you will indeed interview for success!

13

Maxims For Effective Interviewing

The following set of generalizations are based upon various topics discussed in the first twelve chapters. These constitute a handy checklist of "does" and "don'ts" you may want to review just prior to your job interview. Each subject is dealt with more fully in the preceding chapters and can be easily accessed by referring to the index.

1. Interviewing is a communication skill you can successfully learn and apply.

2. How well you interview will influence your present and future salaries as well as your future relationship with the employer.

3. You will conduct several job interviews throughout your worklife, because you will probably change jobs and careers several times.

4. Successful job interview outcomes include both job offers and rejections.

5. Effective job interviews take place after conducting several other job search steps—identifying skills, stating a job objective, writing resumes and letters, conducting job research, and networking.

6. **Preparation** is the key to successful interviewing.

7. You will encounter several types of interviews which require different types of responses—informational, electronic screening, selection/hiring, telephone, one-on-one, sequential, serial, panel, group, or/and stress.

8. Be careful how and what you eat and drink during your interview. Your behavior is being continuously observed.

9. The best jobs with the least competition are found on the **hidden job market**. **Networking** and **informational interviews** are the keys to penetrating the hidden job market.

10. Employers want to hire people who are **competent, intelligent, honest, enthusiastic, friendly, and likable**.

11. If you respond to job listings, you will probably be rejected; your chances of getting an interview are less than 5%.

12. If you want to decrease your percentage of rejections and increase your probability of getting job interviews, you must take the initiative to conduct informational interviews.

13. The best way to get an interview and a job offer is to **never ask for a job**; always ask for information, advice, referrals—and to be remembered for future reference.

14. Most people love to give advice; therefore, your informational interview should be successful.

15. You must be prepared to both answer and ask questions in information and job interviews.

16. In the informational interview, you are the **interviewer**; in the job interview, you are the **interviewee**. Learn to play both roles before engaging in any type of interview.

17. You should always stress your **positives** and **strengths**; never volunteer your negatives.

18. Always send a thank you letter to individuals who helped you in your job search.

19. Approach letters should lead to action by stating a time for arranging an interview.

20. You should look for a job that is **fit for you** (based on your motivated abilities) rather than one that you feel you might fit into.

21. Before going to an interview, research the organization and/or individuals who will interview you.

22. In the end, employers basically hire people they **like**.

23. If asked an illegal question, try to be tactful.

24. Always ask questions about the job during the interview.

25. Keep the salary question to the end of the interview after you have established your **value**. It is preferable to have the interviewer initiate the salary question.

26. Practice interview questions with a friend and tape recorder.

27. Most interviewers make their decision on candidates during the first five minutes of the interview. Therefore, first impressions—both verbal and nonverbal—count a great deal in the job interview.

28. The way you dress will influence the outcome of the interview. As you interview for success, you also should dress for success.

29. Your **color combinations** can make a difference in communicating positive things about you during the interview.

30. Poor grooming in the interview will eliminate you from further consideration for a job.

31. Arrive at the interview site 10-15 minutes ahead of the scheduled interview; never arrive late or too early.

32. Be nice to secretaries and receptionists; the boss often listens to their evaluations of candidates.

33. When waiting for the interviewer to greet you, be seen reading something relevant to the position.

34. You can minimize your nervousness by taking a deep breath and focusing your attention on what is being said.

35. During the interview, you should sit with a slight forward lean, make eye contact frequently, smile moderately, and convey interest through your vocal inflections.

36. Listen carefully to the interviewer as well as give him or her positive nonverbal feedback while listening.

37. Employers want to hear you talk about yourself and the job.

38. Hiring is a risky and expensive business for employers.

39. Employers want to know your **weaknesses**; you should stress your **strengths**.

40. Most interviews follow a questioning sequence that you should be prepared to address.

41. When addressing the interviewer's questions, always use **positive form** and **content** as well as **supports** for your qualifications/accomplishments.

42. Avoid negative terms and comments when responding to questions. Always stress positives.

43. Take some initiative during the interview but don't try to control it.

44. Discuss salary only after you have established your **value**, which will usually be near the end of the interview or after a job offer has been made.

45. Salaries normally are **negotiable**.

46. If you can't reach agreement on a salary figure, try to negotiate other terms of employment, such as special benefits, new job description, promise to reconsider your salary in 6 months.

47. While most employers will not try to exploit you with low salary offers, neither are they eager to pay you more than you are willing to accept. Therefore, do not be too eager to accept the employer's first offer.

48. Salaries are normally assigned to **positions** rather than to individuals. Your task is to negotiate a higher salary, because you as an **individual** will perform better than the average person in the position.

49. Never immediately accept a salary offer. Sleep on it for 24-48 hours during which time you should consider your options.

50. In salary negotiations, you are doing **business**—your talent for the employer's money. It is best to treat it as a business transaction.

51. Your basic goal in salary negotiations is **cash**, not benefits. Benefits tend to be standard—come with the job regardless of your negotiating ability.

52. When closing the interview, take the initiative to **summarize** your strengths and value for the employer and to ask when you might expect to hear the final decision.

53. You should **implement** your job search by developing action plans and following through.

54. You never get a second chance to make a good first impression.

As you read these maxims they should serve to review and reinforce the information presented in greater detail in the first twelve chapters of this book. You may wish to highlight the ones you believe are the most important for you and quickly review those particular ones the morning of your interview as you prepare to interview for success!

Approach Letters

The following approach letters are used as part of a networking and informational interviewing strategy as outlined in Chapter 6. The examples are aimed at two different audiences—personal contacts and strangers. The first eight letters are written via personal contacts. In the final seven examples, the writers are approaching individuals without prior contacts—the classic cold calling situation. In both cases the writers emphasize they are seeking information—not a job—and they take the initiative to telephone the individual in order to make an appointment for an informational interview.

Do not enclose a copy of your resume with an approach letter. The purpose of this letter is to invite yourself to an interview where you will seek information, advice, and referrals. If you enclose a resume, you send the wrong message—you want the person to find you a job.

Referral

821 Stevens Point
Boston, MA 01990

April 14, 19___

Terri Fulton
Director of Personnel
TRS CORPORATION
6311 W. Dover
Boston, MA 01991

Dear Ms. Fulton:

Alice O'Brien suggested that I contact you about my interest in personnel management. She said you are one of the best people to talk to in regard to careers in personnel.

I am leaving government after seven years of increasingly responsible experience in personnel. I am especially interested in working with a large private firm. However, before I venture further into the job market, I want to benefit from the experience and knowledge of others in the field who might advise me on opportunities for someone with my qualifications.

Perhaps we could meet briefly sometime during the next two weeks to discuss my career plans. I have several questions which I believe you could help clarify. I will call your office on Tuesday, April 22, to schedule a meeting time.

I look forward to discussing my plans with you.

Sincerely,

Katherine Kelly

Katherine Kelly

Referral
(possible opening)

9855 Little Glen Court
Dallas, TX 75207

June 23, 19___

Ida Stonewall
PACIFIC DESIGN CENTER
7008 Melrose Avenue
Los Angeles, CA 90069

Dear Ms. Stonewall:

A mutual friend of ours, Tina McGreggor at the Southwest Interior Design Center in Phoenix, suggested I write to you.

I have just completed the requirements for my M.B.A. degree from the University of Texas. As an undergraduate I had the opportunity to work as a co-operative education student in the administrative offices of the Dallas Design Center. I enjoyed my work there and want to explore the possibility of combining my business management training with my interest in design.

I will be returning to my family's home in Santa Monica next month. Tina indicated you would be one of the best people I could talk to regarding the kind of opportunities in the Los Angeles area for someone who was interested in work in one of the area design centers. She said your overview would help get me pointed in the right direction!

I will call you next week to see whether we could schedule a meeting during the week of July 10th. I would truly appreciate it if you could take time out from your busy schedule to meet with me.

Sincerely,

JoAnne McGrosney

JoAnne McGrosney

Referral
(information and advice)

1099 Seventh Avenue
Akron, OH 44522

December 10, 19__

Janet L. Cooper, Director
Architectural Design Office
RT ENGINEERING ASSOCIATES
621 West Grand Avenue
Akron, OH 44520

Dear Ms. Cooper:

John Sayres suggested that I write to you regarding my interest in architectural drafting. He thought you would be a good person to give me some career advice.

I am interested in an architectural drafting position with a firm specializing in commercial construction. As a trained draftsman, I have six years of progressive experience in all facets of construction, from pouring concrete to developing plans for $14 million in commercial and residential construction. I am particularly interested in improving construction design and building operations of shopping complexes.

Mr. Sayres mentioned you as one of the leading experts in this growing field. Would it be possible for us to meet briefly? Over the next few months I will be conducting a job search. I am certain your counsel would assist me as I begin looking for new opportunities.

I will call your office next week to see if your schedule permits such a meeting.

Sincerely,

John Albert

John Albert

Referral
(information and advice)

235 W. Charles St.
Baltimore, MD 21200

July 26, 19___

Craig Allen
T. ROWE PRICE ASSOCIATES, INC.
100 East Pratt Street
Baltimore, MD 21202

Dear Mr. Allen:

Jerry Weitz recommended that I contact you about my interests in Graphic Design. He spoke highly of you and said you might be able to give me some useful advice on job opportunities for someone with my background and interests.

Two years ago I completed my Bachelor's degree in Graphic Design. Since then I've been working as a graphic designer at L. C. Printing Company where I've acquired invaluable experience in all phases of graphic design and production. I have a working knowledge of offset printing and have worked extensively with the MacIntoch Computer and QuarkXPress software.

Mr. Weitz said you have been working with one of the country's leading investment firms during the past seven years as a publications oriented graphic designer. I'm interested in learning more about career opportunities with corporations seeking to develop in-house graphic design capabilities. Would it be possible to meet briefly to discuss my career interests? Since my experience has been limited to the printing industry, I'm sure I could learn a great deal from you.

I'll call you on Wednesday afternoon to see if your schedule would permit such a meeting. I really appreciate whatever information and advice you could give me.

Sincerely,

Laura Baker

Laura Baker

Referral
(information and advice)

SAMUAL ROLLINS

782 N. Davis	Raleigh, NC 27832	831/782-4813

June 28, 19___

Janet O'Brien
JAMES, ALLEN, AND O'BRIEN
8132 Broadway
Washington, DC 20031

Dear Ms. O'Brien:

Mary Varner recommended that I contact you concerning my plans to relocate to the Washington, D.C. area. She said you would be a good person to talk with concerning my interests in contacting firms specializing in environmental law.

While completing my law degree at Emory University, I became very interested in environmental law. Many of the cases I reviewed involved law firms, lobbyists, nonprofit environmental groups, and federal agencies located in Washington, D.C. Not surprising, I concluded the nation's capital is obviously the center for anyone interested in pursuing a career in environmental law.

I'll be visiting Washington the week of July 23. Would it be possible to get together briefly to discuss my career interests. I know I could learn a great deal from your experience and would appreciate any information, advice, and referrals you might give me on opportunities in environmental law. I'll call you next Thursday to see if your schedule would permit such a meeting.

I look forward to meeting you.

Sincerely,

Samuel Rollins

Samuel Rollins

Referral
(information and advice)

4563 Southshore Drive
Key Biscayne, FL 33455

April 15, 19___

Marlo Sikes
Public Relations Director
DOLPHIN CRUISE LINE
873 North American Way
Miami, FL 33132

Dear Ms. Sikes:

Mr. Gerald Barnes of the Cruiseline Travel School, where I am a student, suggested I contact you for information regarding careers in the cruise industry. I will be completing my coursework here next month and am seeking information about opportunities in the travel industry in general and the cruiselines in particular. Mr. Barnes indicated you are one of the best sources of information as to the directions the cruise business is taking and that your network of persons involved in the business is the best of any around.

I realize your schedule is hectic, but I hope you will be able to help me by taking a half-hour of your time to meet with me to share your valuable information and insights into the cruise business with me.

I will call you next Monday to arrange a meeting at a time convenient for you. I truly will appreciate your assistance at this important juncture in plotting my future career.

Sincerely,

Miriam Jordan

Miriam Jordan

Referral
(possible opening)

485 High Bluff Road
Santa Fe, NM 89543

October 3, 19___

Rebecca Lyons
WESTERN INDUSTRIES, INC.
98347 W. Main Street
Albuquerque, NM 89977

Dear Mrs. Lyons:

Cynthia Pringle, my current supervisor and an acquaintance of yours, suggested I write to you. I will be relocating to Albuquerque within the next six weeks and will be looking for employment as a secretary. Cynthia indicated your firm is frequently in need of dependable and competent people to fill vacancies.

I have worked for Cynthia for the past three years and have consistently received "outstanding" ratings in all areas on my performance evaluations. I get along well with people and look forward to beginning work in a new firm in my new city.

I will be driving into Albuquerque the week of the 15th and hope I might be able to meet with you at that time. Even if you do not have a vacancy or anticipate one at this time, I would appreciate the opportunity to talk with you about other contacts I might make to further my job search in Albuquerque.

I will call you next week and hope we may be able to schedule a meeting. I will appreciate any assistance you may be able to give me and look forward to meeting you. Cynthia speaks so highly of you that I know your assistance would be truly valuable to me.

Sincerely,

Karen Jostney

Karen Jostney

Referral
(possible opening)

650 Candlestick Lane
Orem, UT 80933
February 11, 19___

Jack Daniels
SUCCESS SEMINARS, INC.
19788 Expert Lane
Provo, UT 81566

Dear Mr. Daniels:

Jeff Holser, one of your former instructors, suggested that I contact you. He indicated that since your firm has been experiencing rapid growth, you would be a logical person for me to talk with regarding possible training opportunities with Success Seminars, Inc.

After teaching writing courses at Brigham Young University for eight years, I resigned to conduct training seminars for Write To The Point, Inc. and have been with them for the past three years. I like the travel opportunities involved in conducting training seminars across the country and enjoy working with the adult participants.

After twenty-five years offering training seminars, Write To The Point will be closing its doors since its owner is retiring from the business and has chosen to close rather than sell the business. Hence I am looking for opportunities to put my skills to work with another training firm. Jeff has spoken highly of your firm and the outstanding work that you do.

Some of my accomplishments with my present employer include:

- rated as "outstanding" instructor by 92% of seminar participants
- increased sales of tapes and books sold at seminars by over 50%
- 62% of participants who attend my seminars sign up for another seminar within six months

I would appreciate the opportunity to talk with you about your organization as well as possible ways we might work together. I will call you next Monday to schedule an appointment at a mutually convenient time. Thank you for your consideration.

Sincerely,

Bruce Italk

Bruce Italk

Cold Turkey
(information and advice)

2189 West Church Street
New York, NY 10011

May 3, 19____

Patricia Dotson, Director
NORTHEAST ASSOCIATION
   FOR THE ELDERLY
9930 Jefferson Street
New York, NY 10013

Dear Ms. Dotson:

I have been impressed with your work with the elderly. Your organization takes a community perspective in trying to integrate the concerns of the elderly with those of other community groups. Perhaps other organizations will soon follow your lead.

I am anxious to meet you and learn more about your work. My background with the city Volunteer Services Program involved frequent contact with elderly volunteers. From this experience I decided I preferred working primarily with the elderly.

However, before I pursue my interest further, I need to talk to people with experience in gerontology. In particular, I would like to know more about careers with the elderly as well as how my background might best be used in the field of gerontology.

I am hoping you can assist me in this matter. I would like to meet with you briefly to discuss several of my concerns. I will call next week to see if your schedule permits such a meeting.

I look forward to meeting you.

Sincerely,

Carol Timms

Carol Timms

Cold Turkey
(information and advice)

136 West Davis St.
Washington, DC 20030

October 2, 19___

Sharon T. Avery
Vice President for Sales
BENTLEY ENTERPRISES
529 W. Sheridan Road
Washington, DC 20011

Dear Ms. Avery:

I am writing to you because you know the importance of having a knowledgeable, highly motivated, and enthusiastic sales force market your fine information processing equipment. I know because I have been impressed with your sales representatives.

I am seeking your advice on how I might prepare for a career in your field. I have a sales and secretarial background—experience acquired while earning may way through college.

Within the coming months I hope to begin a new career. My familiarity with word processing equipment, my sales experience, and my Bachelor's degree in communication have prepared me for the information processing field. I want to begin in sales and eventually move into a management level position.

As I begin my job search, I am trying to gather as much information and advice as possible before applying for positions. Could I take a few minutes of your time next week to discuss my career plans? Perhaps you could suggest how I can improve my resume—which I am now drafting—and who might be interested in my qualifications. I will call you on Monday to see if such a meeting can be arranged.

I appreciate your consideration and look forward to meeting you.

Sincerely,

Gail S. Topper

Gail S. Topper

Cold Turkey
(information and advice)

4183 Waupelani Drive
State College, PA 16808

October 26, 19___

Dr. Harold Selnik, Chair
Department of Speech Communication
UNIVERSITY OF PITTSBURGH
Pittsburgh, PA 12511

Dear Dr. Selnik:

I was fortunate to have been in the audience this past May when you gave the keynote speech at the Speech Communication Association Convention. Not only did your talk hold the entire audience spellbound, but I found your analysis of the future direction of our field to be the most insightful I have encountered.

I am completing the requirements for my Ph.D. in Communication at Penn State and will be graduated in May. I have not yet decided whether I would prefer to teach or use my background in Communication in another arena. Having heard you speak, I am certain your insights would be helpful to me as I consider this decision.

I will be in Pittsburgh over the Thanksgiving holiday. I hope that your schedule will permit you to meet briefly with me during that time. In fact, I could arrange my schedule to be in Pittsburgh a day before or after your holiday break at the University of Pittsburgh if that would be the most convenient for you.

I will call you next week. I hope we can schedule a meeting at a mutually convenient time. I value your opinions and feel certain that talking with you will enable me to better plan my future in Communication.

Sincerely,

Julie McGuire

Julie McGuire

Cold Turkey
(information and advice)

MARTIN L. POTTER

632 Old Gates Rd.	Landover, MD 23219	410/392-9231

March 17, 19___

Thomas Nelson
ACT TRAINING SYSTEMS
719 Wilson Blvd.
Arlington, VA 21313

Dear Mr. Nelson:

As a fellow member of the American Society For Training and Development, I've admired your work in expanding the involvement of technical trainers in our local ASTD chapter. Indeed, our April symposium on "Developing Needs Assessment in Technical Training" was one of the most useful meetings I've ever attended. It gave me several new ideas I've been able to incorporate in my own professional development.

During the past five years I've been working as a technical trainer with the Department of Navy. I specialize in computer programming of communication systems. While I've very much enjoyed my work with the Navy, it's now time I begin looking at career options in the private sector. I'm especially interested in working with a small consulting firm—preferably one which does contact work with the government—specializing in technical training.

Would your schedule during the next few weeks permit a few minutes to meet with me to discuss my career interests? Having been out of the job market for several years, I would value your advice on how I might best approach the private sector with my technical training interests and skills.

I'll call your office on Thursday afternoon to see if such a meeting would be possible.

Sincerely,

Geraldine West

Geraldine West

Cold Turkey
(information and advice)

9231 Taylor Avenue
Cincinnati, OH 43821

February 3, 19___

Marsha Sullivan, Director
COMMUNITY ACTION FOR SENIORS
812 Fairview Blvd., Suite 201
Cincinnati, OH 43820

Dear Ms. Sullivan:

Congratulations on receiving the annual Jaycee's Community Service Award for your work in developing recreational facilities for the elderly. I've been especially impressed with the new recreational center you helped develop at Siedler Park. It's been a wonderful success, one which many other communities should look to for new ideas.

I'm writing to you because you are experienced in working with the elderly on recreational issues. During the past three years I've been completing my Master's degree in social work while teaching full-time at Wallace High School. I'm planning to leave teaching next year to pursue a career with community-based programs for the elderly.

My long-term career interests are in gerontology. While working on my Master's thesis—"Recreational Options for the Elderly: A Comparison of Three Innovative Community Programs"—I became very interested in working with local recreation programs. I'm now committed to pursuing a career relating to recreation and the elderly.

I would appreciate an opportunity to speak with you about your work in this field. At this stage I'm trying to learn as much as possible about career opportunities relating to recreation involving the elderly. Perhaps you could advise me on where and how I should best focus my job search.

I'll call your office next week to see if your schedule would permit a brief meeting to discuss my career interests. I would appreciate any information, advice, or tips you might provide me at this stage of my job search.

Sincerely,

Margaret Allen

Margaret Allen

Cold Turkey
(possible opening)

5680 Citrine Blvd.
Pekin, IL 61559
March 1, 19___

John Dingle, Manager
PEORIA GAZETTE
13 Walsh Street
Peoria, IL 61564

Dear Mr. Dingle:

I have five years experience as the Personnel Director at the <u>Pekin Times</u>. I have learned a great deal and contributed much during that time, and now would like to move to a position with a larger organization. While at the <u>Times</u>, I have learned specifically about personnel situations that are unique to the publishing business. It is for that reason that I would like to move to another news organization even though I realize that my personnel experience could be useful in many other businesses as well.

The <u>Pekin Times</u> has been leader in personnel innovations which have enabled me to put into place new policies which have been credited with increasing productivity and cutting costs while maintaining customer satisfaction. Highlights of my accomplishments include:

- Saved 20% in medical premiums by instituting programs to improve employee health.
- Reduced employee turnover by 18% through more carefully screening of job applicants and training new employees.
- Reduced employee absenteeism by 11% through coordinated handling of employee complaints by both Personnel and Department Managers.

I would appreciate the opportunity to talk with you about the directions you are headed at the <u>Peoria Gazette</u>. Whether or not we find that there might be an opportunity for me to work in your organization in the future, I think a meeting could be productive for both of us.

I will call you next week to schedule a meeting at your convenience.

Sincerely,

Jack Fielding

Jack Fielding

Cold Turkey
(possible opening)

327 Saffron Court
Pensacola, Fl 33218
January 8, 19___

Darlene Textron, Editor
HONOLULU STAR BULLETIN
87 Lafayette Square
Honolulu, HI 96829

Dear Mrs. Textron:

For the past two years I have been a copywriter for the <u>Pensacola News-Journal</u>. I have found my time in this position to be both productive and enjoyable. I love writing for the newspaper!

I will be making a permanent move to Honolulu in early April and hope to continue to work in the news department for a major newspaper. I believe the <u>Honolulu Star Bulletin</u> would be a good fit for my interest and skills. As you can see from the resume I enclose, I was graduated from the University of Missouri with a double major in journalism and communication. The combination of my formal training with the excellent experience I have had at the <u>Pensacola News-Journal</u> have provided me with a solid background to become a contributing member of another news team. I have been fortunate here to have had the opportunity to work with and learn from some of the best newspeople in Florida. In fact, I was honored to be awarded the certificate of achievement as best copywriter in Northwest Florida at our regional meeting last month.

I will visit Honolulu early next month to make arrangements for housing and also plan to make contacts with various news organizations. I would like very much to talk with you about possible opportunities with the <u>Honolulu Star Bulletin</u>. I realize that you may not have a position open at present, but I believe it could be in the best interests of both of us to explore possible avenues that might be open in the future.

I will call you next week to see whether we might be able to meet briefly while I am in Honolulu. I feel sure I would benefit from having the opportunity to talk with you about the newspaper business in Hawaii.

Sincerely,

Phyllis Jourdan

Phyllis Jourdan

Appendix B

Thank You Letters

T hank you letters can be one of the most effective tools of your job search. The following examples represent different types of thank you letters written in relation to various interview situations. All of the examples represent **thoughtfulness** as well as certain job search objectives.

The **Post-Informational Interview** thank you letter is designed to reinforce two of the major goals of the informational interview—to be referred and remembered.

Post-Job Interview thank you letters should be sent immediately following a job interview. The purpose of these letters is to get the employer to remember your particular strengths and value.

The **Withdraw from Consideration** thank you letter should be sent if you decide to withdraw your application. Briefly indicate the reason for your withdrawal and thank them for their time and consideration. They should remember you favorably if you later wish to be considered for another position.

The **Job Rejection** thank you letter also is designed to stress your strengths and value as well as to get the employer to remember you for future reference. Sometimes these letters can lead to another interview and a job offer with the same employer who has another opening later or to a referral to another employer.

The **Job Offer Acceptance** thank you letter also can be one of the most effective job search letters. Since employers normally do not receive such letters from their new employees and since it is a thoughtful thing to do, such a letter should make a very favorable initial on-the-job impression. The employer will remember you in a positive light.

Post Informational Interview

9910 Thompson Drive
Cleveland, OH 43382

June 21, 19____

Jane Evans, Director
EVANS FINANCE CORPORATION
2122 Forman Street
Cleveland, OH 43380

Dear Ms. Evans:

Your advice was most helpful in clarifying my questions on careers in finance. I am now reworking my resume and have included many of your thoughtful suggestions. I will send you a copy next week.

Thanks so much for taking time from your busy schedule to see me. I will keep in contact and follow through on your suggestion to see Sarah Cook about opportunities with the Cleveland-Akron Finance Company.

Sincerely,

Daryl Haines

Daryl Haines

Post Informational Interview

9855 Little Glen Court
Dallas, TX 75207

July 29, 19____

Ida Stonewall
PACIFIC DESIGN CENTER
7008 Melrose Avenue
Los Angeles, CA 90069

Dear Ms. Stonewall:

Thank you for taking the time to meet with me yesterday. I thoroughly enjoyed our meeting and the information you gave me was most helpful.

I have already contacted three of the people you suggested I should talk with and have appointments to meet with them over the next two weeks. The fourth person, Jerrie Forsythe, is on vacation so I will try to contact her again next week.

I would appreciate it if you would keep me in mind if you talk with someone in the near future who is looking for an individual with credentials similar to mine. Talking with you only made me more anxious to get into a job in a design center.

As you suggested, I will keep in touch with you over the next few weeks and let you know how my job search is going.

Most sincerely,

JoAnne McGrosney

JoAnne McGrosney

Post Informational Interview

4183 Waupelani Drive
State College, PA 16808

December 1, 19__

Dr. Harold Selnik, Chairman
Department of Speech Communication
UNIVERSITY OF PITTSBURGH
Pittsburgh, PA 12511

Dear Dr. Selnik:

Thank you for taking the time to meet with me last Friday. It was most kind of you—especially since you took time from your Thanksgiving break at the university to do so. I found the meeting even more helpful to me than I had anticipated. I had never even considered some of the options open to someone with my major!

I have taken your advice and have made appointments to talk with some of the people whom you suggested. I am sure their advice will also be useful to me.

I will keep in touch with you and let you know what decisions I make and what opportunities I take during the remainder of this year.

Thanks again for helping me make some decisions very important to my future.

Sincerely,

Julie McGuire

Julie McGuire

Post Informational Interview

4563 Southshore Drive
Key Biscayne, FL 33455

May 5, 19___

Marlo Sikes
Public Relations Director
DOLPHIN CRUISE LINE
873 North American Way
Miami, FL 33132

Dear Ms. Sikes:

I am grateful for the opportunity to meet with you today. As Mr. Barnes had indicated, you are certainly one of the best informed persons in the Miami area when it comes to questions about the cruise industry. Your knowledge as well as analysis of future trends is right on the mark, yet I had not looked at it that way before.

My discussion with you helped me focus on the direction I want to pursue. I really believe I would be happier working in a cruiseline's corporate offices rather than taking a job on board ship. You mentioned during our discussion that you would be happy to put me in contact with several people in your network if I decided this was the direction I wished to take.

I am writing to ask your assistance in making contact with these people. I will call you in a few days to get these names and addresses from you. I certainly appreciate this additional assistance on your part.

Thank you again for taking time from your busy schedule to meet with me. I look forward to seeing you again in the future—hopefully when I am working for a cruiseline!

Sincerely,

Julie McGuire

Miriam Jordan

Post Job Interview

2962 Forrest Drive
Denver, CO 82171

May 28, 19___

Thomas F. Harris
Director, Personnel Department
COASTAL PRODUCTS, INC.
7229 Lakewood Drive
Denver, CO 82170

Dear Mr. Harris:

Thank you again for the opportunity to interview for the marketing position. I appreciated your hospitality and enjoyed meeting you and members of your staff.

The interview convinced me of how compatible my background, interests, and skills are with the goals of Coastal Products Incorporated. My prior marketing experience with the Department of Commerce has prepared me to take a major role in developing both domestic and international marketing strategies. I am confident my work could result in increased market shares for Coastal Products Incorporated in the rapidly expanding Pacific Rim market.

For more information on the new product promotion program I mentioned, call David Garrett at the Department of Commerce; his number is 202/726-0132. I talked to Dave this morning and mentioned your interest in this program.

I look forward to meeting you and your staff again.

Sincerely,

Stephanie Potter

Stephanie Potter

Post Job Interview

1947 Grace Avenue
Springfield, MA 01281

November 17, _____

James R. Quinn, Director
Personnel Department
DAVIS ENTERPRISES
2290 Cambridge Street
Boston, MA 01181

Dear Mr. Quinn:

Thank you for the opportunity to interview yesterday for the Sales Trainee position. I enjoyed meeting you and learning more about Davis Enterprises. You have a fine staff and a sophisticated approach to marketing.

Your organization appears to be growing in a direction which parallels my interests and career goals. The interview with you and your staff confirmed my initial positive impressions of Davis Enterprises, and I want to reiterate my strong interest in working for you. My prior experience in operating office equipment plus my training in communication would enable me to progress steadily through your training program and become a productive member of your sales team.

Again, thank you for your consideration. If you need any additional information from me, please feel free to call.

Yours truly,

Gail S. Topper

Gail S. Topper

Post Job Interview

8712 Graham Blvd.
Staunton, VA 23212

January 28, 19___

Edward Jason
Personnel Administrator
CITY OF CHARLESTON
P.O. Box 4561
Charleston, WV 25331

Dear Mr. Jason:

I appreciated the opportunity to interview with you today. Having talked with you and found out in greater depth about the opening you have, I am more sure than ever that I would like to work for the City of Charleston as Parks and Recreation Director.

Having directed all phases of community recreational programs while I was the director in Staunton, I feel certain I could bring the kind of leadership to the program in Charleston that you indicate you need. I also feel certain that under my supervision it would be possible to expand the programs without the need to increase the budget. In these recessionary times that becomes a critical consideration.

I hope to have the opportunity to help Charleston revitalize its recreational programs. Please let me know if I may provide any further information that will be helpful as you make your hiring decision.

I will call you next Friday, as you suggested, to see how your selection process is going.

Sincerely,

Sylvia Whitehurst

Sylvia Whitehurst

Post Job Interview

882 Forest Lane
Cleveland, OH 43210

March 16, 19___

Jonathan Morrison
Circulation Department
CLEVELAND PLAIN DEALER
8250 Lakefront Blvd.
Cleveland, OH 43208

Dear Mr. Morrison:

I really appreciated having the opportunity to interview with you today for the position of Dispatcher. I remain extremely interested in this position. I am especially interested because it is an evening job. I am used to working an evening schedule and feel I might have trouble adapting to a day job.

If I have not heard from you by next Friday, I will check back with you to see how your selection process is progressing. I look forward to hearing from you and hope I will have the opportunity to work with you.

Sincerely,

Jack Diamond

Jack Diamond

Post Job Interview

5680 Citrine Blvd.
Pekin, IL 61559

March 12, 19___

John Dingle
General Manager
PEORIA GAZETTE
13 Walsh Street
Peoria, IL 61564

Dear Mr. Dingle:

I wish to thank you for taking the time to meet with me yesterday. I enjoyed talking with you and finding out more about what is happening at the Peoria Gazette.

I found it fascinating that you are planning to innovate in areas similar to those where we at the Times have made recent changes. I believe I have a lot to offer to the Gazette and ask that you seriously consider me if you decide to restructure and add the new position in Personnel that we talked about. I met several interesting people at lunch with you yesterday and I know I would enjoy working with you and your staff.

I enclose the resume I promised to send you. I will call you in a few days to see whether you have any further questions.

Sincerely,

Jack Fielding

Jack Fielding

Withdrawing From Consideration

3773 Nevada Street
Portland, OR 98677

July 5, 19___

Ann Jenkins
KALIN'S DRESS SHOP
3456 Centre Street
Portland, OR 98678

Dear Mrs. Jenkins:

Thank you for giving me the opportunity to talk with you yesterday about the opening you have for a salesperson at your store.

You were more helpful than you know. I had always thought working in a dress shop would be fun—the chance to work with all those pretty clothes! After talking with you, I realize how much hard work is involved before the clothing makes its way to the racks in the store. I no longer believe this is the right line of work for me. Thank you for helping me make an important decision.

You have a beautiful store and I have no doubt you will have no difficulty finding the right person to fill your sales opening.

Sincerely,

Angelique Martin

Angelique Martin

Withdrawing From Consideration

2345 Glen Echo Court
Berea, OH 44375

October 7, 19___

Dr. Harriet Learner, Chair
Department of Communication
CUYAHOGA COMMUNITY COLLEGE
Cleveland, OH 44452

Dear Dr. Learner:

Thank you for selecting me to interview for the instructor position open in the Communication Department for the coming academic year. I appreciated the opportunity to meet with you and other members of the faculty. You have an outstanding program and it would be a privilege for me to have the opportunity to work with you.

However, I must request that you withdraw my application from further consideration. I have just received an offer from the Leeward Community College in Pearl City, Hawaii, to teach in their Department of Speech Communication. This position will give me the chance to further my study of the linguistic components of Native American speech; I hope to be able to complete the book I am writing within the year.

I know you will have no trouble selecting a competent candidate to fill your opening. I do plan to return to Ohio within a year or two to be closer to my parents, and I hope we may be able to get together again at that time. If you have an opening next year in my areas of specialty, I would very much appreciate hearing about it at that time.

I will keep in touch with you over the next year.

Sincerely,

Marcus McDonald

Marcus McDonald

Withdrawing From Consideration

733 Main Street
Williamsburg, VA 23512

December 1, 19___

Dr. Thomas C. Bostelli, President
NORTHERN STATES UNIVERSITY
2500 University Drive
Greenfield, MA 03241

Dear Dr. Bostelli:

It was indeed a pleasure meeting with you and your staff last week to discuss your need for a Director of Public and Government Relations. Our time together was most enjoyable and informative.

As I discussed with you during our meetings, I believe one purpose of preliminary interviews is to explore areas of mutual interest and to assess the fit between the individual and the position. After careful consideration, I have decided to withdraw from consideration for the position.

My decision is based upon several factors. First, the emphasis on fund raising is certainly needed, but I would prefer more balance in my work activities. Second, the position would require more travel than I am willing to accept with my other responsibilities. Third, professional opportunities for my husband would be very limited in northwest Massachusetts.

I want to thank you for interviewing me and giving me the opportunity to learn about your needs. You have a fine staff and faculty, and I would have enjoyed working with them.

Best wishes in your search.

Sincerely,

Janet L. Lawson

Janet L. Lawson

Responding to Rejection

1947 Grace Avenue
Springfield, MA 01281

September 14, 19___

Sharon T. Avery
Vice President for Sales
BENTLEY ENTERPRISES
529 W. Sheridan Road
Washington, DC 20011

Dear Ms. Avery:

Thank you for giving me the opportunity to interview for the Customer Services Representative position. I appreciate your consideration and interest in me. I learned a great deal from our meetings.

Although I am disappointed in not being selected for your current vacancy, I want you to know that I appreciated the courtesy and professionalism shown to me during the entire selection process. I enjoyed meeting you, John Roberts, and other members of your sales staff. My meetings confirmed that Bentley Enterprises would be an exciting place to work and build a career.

I want to reiterate my strong interest in working for you. Please keep me in mind should another position become available in the near future.

Again, thank you for the opportunity to interview. Best wishes to you and your staff.

Yours truly,

Gail S. Topper

Gail S. Topper

Responding to Rejection

455 Los Altos Drive
Los Angeles, CA 91095

October 24, 19___

Jennifer Strong
THE GREEN BEAN CO.
241 Greenbrier Road
Los Angeles, CA 91093

Dear Mrs. Strong:

I was sorry to hear of the selection of another candidate to fill the slot of manager of the first of three stores you will be opening in the L.A. area. However, I am certain that you had good reasons for the choice you made. My disappointment at not having been selected is someone else's joy.

I know you plan to open two more stores in this area over the next few months. I am writing to request that you keep my resume in an "open" file and reconsider my application for the two other slots as they become available. In fact, I enclose an additional copy of my resume for your convenience.

I have a high regard for your products, think my experience could serve you well and hope to have the opportunity to talk with you again regarding future openings you will have in the L.A. area.

Thank you for your consideration.

Sincerely,

Linda Perry

Linda Perry

Responding to Rejection

781 Humphrey Blvd.
Minneapolis, MN 53821

August 22, 19____

Sandra Delray
OLLEN GRAPHICS
182 Thompson Ave.
Suite 914
Minneapolis, MN 53824

Dear Ms. Delray:

I have just received your letter indicating that another candidate was selected for the position I interviewed for—a graphic artist. Of course I am disappointed, but I am sure you will be pleased with the person you selected.

I wish to take this opportunity to thank you for your consideration. I really appreciated the professional way in which the hiring process was conducted. I enjoyed meeting many of the artists in your firm and believe I would have worked well with them.

Please keep me in mind when you have another opening in your firm. I remain very interested in your company and the fine work you do.

Sincerely,

Debra Summers

Debra Summers

Accepting Job Offer

2589 Jason Drive
Ithaca, NY 14850

August 19, 19___

Sharon A. Waters
Personnel Director
NEW YORK STATE POLICE
Administrative Division
892 South Park
Albany, NY 11081

Dear Ms. Waters:

I want to thank you and Mr. Gordon for giving me the opportunity to work with the New York State Police. I am very pleased to accept the position as a research and data analyst with your planning unit. The position requires exactly the kind of work I want to do, and I know that I will do a good job for you.

As we discussed, I shall begin work on October 1. In the meantime, I shall compete all the necessary employment forms, obtain the required physical examination, and locate housing. I plan to be in Albany within the next two weeks and would like to deliver the paperwork to you personally. At that time we could handle any remaining items pertaining to my employment. I'll call next week to schedule an appointment with you.

I enjoyed my interviews with you and Mr. Gordon and look forward to beginning my job with the Planning Unit.

Sincerely,

Cheryl Ayers

Cheryl Ayers

cc: Mr. Edward Gordon, Administrator
      Planning Unit

Accepting Job Offer

8172 Western Avenue
Cedar Rapids, IA 54019

September 29, 19___

Morris Edelson
ICRW INTERNATIONAL
28 W. 32nd Street
New York, NY 10031

Dear Mr. Edelson:

I was so pleased to receive the job offer from ICRW. I am appreciative of the confidence you have in my work and I will work hard to deserve the support you are giving me. I don't know which I am more excited about—the work I will be doing or the location where I will be working. The chance to work on-site in Indonesia will be extremely interesting.

I look forward to working with you and the staff of ICRW over the coming year.

Sincerely,

Lynne Gardner

Lynne Gardner

Accepting Job Offer

712 W. Vermont St.
Washington, DC 20132

June 10, 19___

Elliott Stevens
WASHINGTON MONTHLY
1611 Connecticut Ave., NW
Washington, DC 20009

Dear Mr. Stevens:

    It is with great anticipation that I accept your offer of a summer internship with the <u>Washington Monthly</u>. I appreciate the confidence that you obviously have in me and promise that I will not disappoint you. I am sure my work with you will help me with my journalism studies when I return to school in the fall.

    I will plan to begin work on the June 21, as we discussed. Please let me know if there is any paperwork I need to complete before reporting to work that day.

Sincerely,

Tracey Nelson

Tracey Nelson

Accepting Job Offer

7694 James Courts
San Francisco, CA 94826

June 7, 19___

Judith Greene
Vice President
WEST COAST AIRLINES
2400 Van Ness
San Francisco, CA 94829

Dear Ms. Greene:

I am pleased to accept your offer, and I am looking forward to joining you and your staff next month.

The customer relations position is ideally suited to my background and interests. I assure you I will give you my best effort in making this an effective position within your company.

I understand I will begin work on July 1. If, in the meantime, I need to complete any paper work or take care of any other matters, please contact me at 377-4029.

I enjoyed meeting with you and your staff and appreciated the professional manner in which the hiring was conducted.

Sincerely,

Joan Kitner

Joan Kitner

Key Career Planning and Job Search Resources

uring the past 20 years hundreds of self-help books have been written on how to find a job and advance one's career. Each year dozens of additional volumes are published to inform as well as enlighten a growing audience of individuals concerned with conducting an effective job search.

In this section we attempt to bring some coherence and organization to this literature to assist you in identifying any additional resources that might be useful to you in developing a successful job search. Most of them go far beyond the job interview. Since some of these resources cannot be found in local bookstores or libraries, you may need to order them directly from the publishers. For your convenience, you can order many of them through Impact Publications by completing the order form at the end of this book or through their on-line bookstore: *http://www.impactpublications.com.*

Choose What's Best For You

You may be initially overwhelmed with the sheer volume of the career planning and job search literature available to help individuals find jobs and change careers. Once you examine a few books, such as this one, you will quickly learn that this literature is designed to be **used**. The books are not intended to describe a subject, explain reality, develop a theory, predict the future, nor entertain you.

Most career planning and job search books attempt to advance self-help **strategies** based upon the particular ideas or experiences of individual writers. They expound a **set of beliefs**—more or less logical and based on a mixture of research, experience, and faith. Like other how-to literature on positive thinking, motivation, and success, you must first **believe** in these books before you can make them work for you. Since the research base for most of these books is very thin, this literature must be primarily judged on the basis of faith and usefulness.

Given the nature of this literature, your best approach is to pick **and choose** which books are **more or less useful** for you. There is nothing magical about these books. At best, they may challenge your preconceptions; develop alternative beliefs which you may or may not find acceptable; provide you with some directions; and help motivate you to implement an effective job search. They will not get you a job.

The level of redundancy in this literature may be disturbing to many readers. More so than in many other fields, career planning writers tend to quote each other or rely on the perspectives of a few key writers in restating the same approaches in a different form. As a result, many individuals confuse the high level of redundancy as repeated evidence of career and job search "facts."

What You Get

We have examined most of the career planning and job search literature with a view toward identifying the best of the lot. We've judged the literature in terms of its degree of accuracy, realism, comprehensiveness, and usefulness. In doing so, we have found three major types of books which use different approaches to getting a job:

- Books designed to teach key job search **process and strategy skills**; these books emphasize "how" questions.

- Books designed to outline various **employment fields**; these books focus on "what" and "where" questions.

- Books designed to address key career issues for **special groups**; these books emphasize "what" and "how" questions.

A growing number of comprehensive job search books attempt to apply the process and strategy skills to different employment fields and special groups.

Process and Strategy Skills

The first type of career planning and job search literature concentrates primarily on developing **process and strategy skills**. Most of these books tell you **how** to develop an effective job search regardless of your particular employment field or your specialized needs. They seldom address substantive **what** and **where** questions central to finding any job. You are left to answer these questions on your own or by using other resources which focus on what jobs are available and where you can find them.

Except for several new books that examine how to find a job by using computers and the Internet, there are few surprises in this literature. Most books follow a similar pattern in approaching the subject. The major difference is that the books are more or less readable. Most of these process books are preoccupied with "getting in touch with yourself" by emphasizing the need to "know what you want to do today, tomorrow, and the rest of your life." Some of this literature is rightly referred to as "touchy-feely" because of its concern with trying to get you to know yourself—the basis for self-assessment. A mainstay of psychologists, counselors, and activity-oriented trainers, this type of positive, up-beat literature is at best designed to reorient your life around

1. identifying what is right about yourself (your strengths), and

2. setting goals based upon an understanding of your past and present in the hope you will do better in the future (your objectives).

The real strengths of this literature lie in orienting your thinking along new lines, providing you with some baseline information on your strengths and goals, and providing you with positive motivation for developing and implementing an effective job search strategy. If you're looking for specifics, such as learning **what** the jobs are and **where** you can find them, this literature may disappoint you with its vagueness.

Placed within our career planning framework in Chapter 6, much of this process and strategy literature falls into the initial two steps of our career planning process: self-assessment and objective setting. Examples of career planning literature using this approach are the popular books written by Bolles, Crystal, Sturman, Miller, Mattson, Tieger, Sher, and Krannich: *Where Do I Go From Here With My Life?*, *What Color Is Your Parachute?*, *The Three Boxes of Life*, *Career Discovery Project*, *The Truth About You*, *Do What You Are*, *I Could Do Anything If I Only Knew What It Was*, *Wishcraft*, *Discover the Best Jobs For You*, *The Pathfinder*, and *Me, Myself, and I, Inc*. You should read these books if you lack a clear understanding of who you are, what you want to do, and where you are going. They may help you get in touch with yourself before you get in touch with employers! If these self-discovery books don't deliver with such self-understanding, you probably need to see a professional counselor who can administer tests as well as walk you through a comprehensive self-assessment process.

Several books focus on additional steps in the career planning and job search processes, such as doing research, writing resumes and letters, networking, interviewing, and negotiating salary. While also emphasizing process and strategy, these are more comprehensive books than the others. Some books include all of the job search steps whereas others concentrate on one or two major steps. Examples of the most comprehensive such books include those by Krannich, Kennedy and Laramore, Lathrop, Jackson, Figler, Yate, Studner, and Wendleton: *Change Your Job Change Your Life*, *Joyce Lain Kennedy's Career Book*, *Who's Hiring Who*, *The Complete Job Search Handbook*, *Guerrilla Tactics in the New Job Market*, *Through the Brick Wall*, *Knock 'Em Dead*, and *Super Job Search*.

You will find hundreds of books that focus on the **research stage** of the job search. Except for Crowther's *Researching Your Way to a Good Job*, most of these books are geographic, field, or organizational directories or job banks which list names and addresses of potential employers. Examples include the Adams Media's *Job Bank Series* on 31 major cities and metropolitan areas; Surrey Book's *How to Get a Job in...* series on seven cities; Wright's *The American Almanac of Jobs and Salaries*; Schwartz's and Brechner's *The Career Finder;* Krantz's *The Jobs Rated Almanac*; Hoover's *500*, Hoover's *Handbook of World Business*, and *Hoover's Handbook of Emerging Companies*; Lauber's *Government Job Finder, Professional's Job Finder*, and *Non-Profits' and Education Job Finder*; Kennedy Publications' *Directory of Execu-*

tive Recruiters; Adams Media's *National Job Bank* and *Job Bank Guide to Employment Services*; Ferguson's *Encyclopedia of Careers and Vocational Guidance*; Dun and Bradstreet's *The Career Guide: Dun's Employment Opportunity Directory*; and the Department of Labor's *Occupational Outlook Handbook* and *The Dictionary of Occupational Titles* and the *O*NET Dictionary of Occupational Titles*. Job search approaches relating to much of this literature are in sharp contrast to approaches of the standard career planning literature. Directories, for example, should be used to gather information—names, addresses, and phone numbers—to be used in targeting one's networking activities rather than as sources for shotgunning resumes and letters.

Numerous books are written on other key job search steps—especially resume and letter writing and job interviews. The **resume and letter writing** books fall into two major categories:

- Books designed to walk you through the process of developing resumes and letters based upon a thorough understanding of each step in the job search process. Examples include Krannich's and Banis' *High Impact Resumes and Letters*, Jackson's *The New Perfect Resume*, Good's *Does Your Resume Wear Blue Jeans?*, Swanson's *The Resume Solution*, and Beatty's *The Perfect Cover Letter*.

- Books primarily presenting examples of resumes and letters. Examples of such books are numerous—most resume books you will find in libraries and bookstores fall in this category. Some of better such books include Enelow's *100 Winning Resumes For $100,000+ Jobs, 201 Winning Cover Letters For $100,000+ Jobs*; and *1500+ KeyWords For $100,000+ Jobs*; Parker's *Resume Catalog;* Kaplan's *Resume Shortcuts, Sure-Hire Resumes*, and *101 Resumes For Sure-Hire Results,* Adams Media's *The Adams Resume Almanac*; Farr's *America's Top Resumes For America's Top Jobs*; Marino's *Just Resumes;* Jacksons' *Perfect Resume Strategies*; Fournier's and Spin's *Encyclopedia of Job-Winning Resumes;* Career Press's *Resumes Resumes Resumes*; Noble's *The Gallery of Best Resumes*; Frank's *200 Letters For Job Hunters;* Krannichs' *201 Dynamite Job Search Letters*; Kay's *Cover Letters That Will Get You the Job You Want*, and Beatty's *175 High-Impact Cover Letters*.

The first type of resume and letter writing book urges the user to develop resumes and letters that represent the "unique you" in relation to specific positions and employers. They further emphasize the importance of finding a job that is right for you rather than try to adjust your experience to fit into a job that may be inappropriate for you. These books are based upon a particular approach to finding a job as outlined in several of the comprehensive career planning and job search books.

The second type of resume and letter writing book lacks a clear approach other than an implied suggestion that readers should creatively plagiarize the examples. In other words, good resumes and letters are produced by osmosis! A few resume and letter writing books, such as Parker's *The Damn Good Resume Guide*, Schuman's and Lewis' *Revising Your Resume*, Beatty's *The Resume Kit*, Coxford's *Resume Writing Made Easy*, the Krannichs' *Dynamite Resumes* and *Dynamite Cover Letters*, Kennedy's *Resumes For Dummies*, Yates' *Resumes That Knock 'Em Dead*, and *Cover Letters That Knock 'Em Dead* fall between these two types. Several new resume books now focus on developing electronic resumes appropriate for resume databases and the Internet: Kennedy's *Electronic Resume Revolution*, Weddle's *Internet Resumes*, Criscito's *Resumes in Cyberspace*, and Gonyea's *Electronic Resumes: Putting Your Resume On-Line*.

Several books address the issue of **networking** in the job search. A few books focus on job search networking—Krannichs' *Dynamite Networking For Dynamite Jobs*, Lowstuter and Robertson's *Network Your Way to Your Next Job*, National Business Employment Weekly's *Networking*, and Beatty's *Job Search Networking*. Boe and Youngs' *Is Your "Net" Working?* and Garnas' *How to Use People and Get What You Want—and Still Be a Nice Guy!* look at how to build contacts for career development. Baber's and Waymon's *Great Connections*, and RoAne's *How to Work a Room*, *What Do I Say Next?*, and *Secrets of Savvy Networking*; Mandel's *Power Schmoozing*; and Boylan's *The Power to Get In* examine the small talk phenomenon that is the key to developing networks in career, business, and social situations. Donna and Sandy Vilas' *Power Networking* outlines 55 networking methods for achieving success.

You will also find several **job interview** books designed for both interviewees and interviewers. Most of these books examine each step in the interview process—from preparation to negotiating salary. Interview books such as the Krannichs' *Interview For Success* look at each step of the interview process within a well defined career development and job search process. Some interview books, such as DeLuca's Best *Answers to 201 Most Frequently Asked Interview Questions*, Allen's *The Complete Q & A Job Interview Book*, and Fry's *101 Great Answers to the Toughest Interview Questions,* focus primarily on questions and answers. Other interview books, such as the Krannich's *101 Dynamite Answers to Interview Questions* and Kay's *Interview Strategies That Will Get You the Job You Want* are more comprehensive, including interview settings, types of interviews, and nonverbal communication along with a discussion of appropriate questions and answers. Some other good interview books are written by Fein, Kennedy, Schmidt, Medley, Washington, Farr, and the National Business Employment Weekly: *101 Dynamite Questions to Ask At Your Job Interview, 111 Dynamite Ways to Ace Your Job Interview, Job Interviews For Dummies, The 90-Minute Interview Prep Book, Sweaty Palms, Interview Power, The Quick Interview and Salary Negotiation Book*, and *NBEW's Interviewing*.

While most comprehensive job search and interview books include a section on **salary negotiations**, a few books have been written specifically on this subject. The Krannichs' *Dynamite Salary Negotiations: Know What You're Worth and Get It!* and *Get a Raise in 7 Days* examine salary negotiation strategies as well as data on salary ranges. Simon's *Negotiate Your Job Offer* and Miller's *Get More Money On Your Next Job* also examine the whole process of negotiating salaries. Despite its title, Chapman's *How to Make $1,000 a Minute,* also examines salary negotiation strategies. Much of the general literature on negotiation tactics is relevant to this topic.

A final set of "process" books focus on **using computers and the Internet** for finding a job. Most of these books attempt to sort through the newly emerging, and extremely chaotic, electronic job market as well as examine how to use the latest electronic technology for locating job listings and transmitting electronic resumes to online bulletin boards and databases. These books represent high-tech approaches to quickly exploring classified ads and vacancy announcements, networking for information and advice, and broadcasting resumes and letters to numerous employers. Some of the best books exploring this arena include Kennedy's *Electronic Resume Revolution* and *Hook Up, Get Hired*, Dixon's and Tiersten's *Be Your Own Headhunter Online*, Glossbrenner's *Finding a Job on the Internet*, Gonyea's *The On-Line Job Search Companion*, Godin's *Point and Click Jobfinder*, Riley's *The*

Guide to Internet Job Searching, Jandt's and Nemnich's *Using the Internet and the World Wide Web in Your Job Search*, Crispin's and Mehler's *CareerXroads*, and the Karls' *How to Get Your Dream Job Using the Web*.

Specific Employment Fields

A second type of career and job search literature focuses primarily on specific employment fields. These books come in many forms. Some are designed to give the reader a general overview of what type of work is involved in each field. Other books include educational training and job search strategies appropriate for entry into each field. And still others are annotated listings of job and career titles—the most comprehensive being the Department of Labor's *Occupational Outlook Handbook*, *The Dictionary of Occupational Titles*, and the *O'NET Dictionary of Occupational Titles*; *Jobs 1998*; Krantz's *Jobs Rated Almanac* and *The World Almanac Job Finder's Guide*; and Wright's *The American Almanac of Jobs and Salaries*. A few books attempt to link self-assessment data on individual values, interests, and skills to specific employment fields: *Guide For Occupational Exploration*, *The Enhanced Guide For Occupational Exploration*, and *Exploring Careers*.

The majority of books on employment fields are designed for individuals who are considering a particular employment field rather than for individuals wishing to advance within a field. As such, most of these books are general introductions designed to answer important "what," "where," and "how" questions for high school and college students. They provide little useful information for older and more experienced professionals who need more detailed and advanced information on their specific employment field. Examples of such books include 180 volumes in NTC Publishing's *Opportunities in... Series* with such titles as *Opportunities in Architecture, Opportunities in Office Occupations, Opportunities in Public Relations, Opportunities in Forestry*, and *Opportunities in Travel Careers*. More and more books are being produced in specific employment fields, especially for computer, business, accounting, medical, government, international, communication, media, and travel specialists.

Specialized Career Groups

A final set of career planning and job search books has emerged during the past few years. These books are designed for specific groups of job seekers who supposedly need specialized assistance not found in most general job search process and employment field books. The most common such books focus on women, minorities, the handicapped, immigrants, public employees, military personnel, educators, mobile spouses, college graduates, gays, children, and teenagers.

Many of these books represent a new type of career planning book that will most likely continue to appear in the foreseeable future. Several books deal with both **process** and **substance**. They link the substantive "what" and "where" concerns of specific employment fields to "how" processes appropriately outlined for each field.

Take, for example, the field of advertising. Several books, such as Caffrey's *So You Want to Be in Advertising*, Mogal's *Making It in the Media Professions,* and Morgan's *The Advertising Career Directory* outline the jobs available in the field of advertising (what questions); where you should look for vacancies (where questions); and the best strategies for finding a job, including resumes, letters, and interview questions appropriate for the advertising field (how questions).

These specialized career books finally identify how general job search strategies must be adapted and modified to respond to the employment needs of different types of individuals as well as to the employment cultures found in different fields. Some of the most popular such books include *The Minority Career Handbook, Job Strategies For People With Disabilities, The Complete Guide to Public Employment, The Complete Guide to International Jobs and Careers, Flying High in Travel, Educator's Guide to Alternative Jobs and Careers, The New Relocating Spouse's Guide to Employment, Summer Opportunities For Kids and Teenagers, Job Opportunities in Health Care,* and *Environmental Jobs For Scientists and Engineers.*

In the coming decade we can expect to see many more career planning books produced along these combined process, field, and specialized group lines. While general career planning books focusing only on process and strategy will continue to proliferate, the real excitement in this field will be centered around the continuing development of books which link the job search and career planning processes to specific employment fields and specialized groups. If, for example, you are in the fields of real estate or robotics, you should be able to find books outlining what the jobs are, where to find them, and how to get them. Such books will most likely be written by seasoned professionals who represent specialized groups rather than by career planning professionals who are primarily trained in process skills. Such books will meet a growing need for information from individuals who have a solid understanding of how to get a job based on familiarity with the "ins" and "outs" of each field.

The following bibliography includes some of the best career planning resources available today. Consistent with the structure of this book and our discussion of the career and job literature, we have organized the bibliography according to process, field, and group categories.

Bibliography

Job Search Strategies and Tactics

Bolles, Richard N., *What Color Is Your Parachute?* (Berkeley, CA: Ten Speed Press, annual)

Elderkin, Kenton W., *How to Get Interviews From Classified Job Ads* (Manassas Park, VA: Impact Publications, 1993)

Figler, Howard E., *The Complete Job Search Handbook* (New York: Holt, Rinehart, and Winston, 1988)

Godin, Seth, *Point & Click Job Finder* (Chicago: Dearborn, 1996)

Gonyea, James C., *The On-Line Job Search Companion* (New York: McGraw-Hill, 1995)

Hartman, Julia, *Strategic Job Jumping* (Sacramento, CA: Prima, 1997)

Jackson, Tom, *Guerrilla Tactics in the New Job Market* (New York: Bantam, 1991)

Jandt, Fred E. and Mary B. Nemnich, *Using the Internet and the World Wide Web in Your Job Search* (Indianapolis, IN: JIST Works, 1997)

Kennedy, Joyce Lain, *Hook Up, Get Hired* (New York: Wiley, 1995)

Kennedy, Joyce Lain and Darryl Laramore, *Joyce Lain Kennedy's Career Book* (Lincolnwood, IL: NTC Publishing, 1996)

Kennedy, Joyce Lain and Thomas J. Morrow, *Electronic Job Search Revolution* (New York: Wiley, 1995)

Krannich, Ronald L., *Change Your Job, Change Your Life* (Manassas Park, VA, Impact Publications, 1997)

Lathrop, Richard, *Who's Hiring Who* (Berkeley, CA: Ten Speed Press, 1989)

Lucht, John, *The New Rites of Passage at $100,000+* (New York: Henry Holt, 1993)

Riley, Margaret, Frances Roehm, and Steve Oserman, *The Guide to Internet Job Searching* (Lincolnwood, IL: NTC Publishing, 1998)

Siegel, Barbara and Robert Siegel, *The Five Secrets to Finding a Job* (Manassas Park, VA: Impact Publications, 1994)

Studner, Peter K., *Super Job Search* (Los Angeles, CA: Jamenair Ltd., 1996)

Yate, Martin, *Knock 'Em Dead* (Boston, MA: Adams Media, 1997)

Wendleton, Kate, *Through the Brick Wall* (New York: Villard Books, 1992)

Skills Identification, Testing, and Self-Assessment

Bolles, Richard N., *The New Quick Job Hunting Map* (Berkeley, CA: Ten Speed Press, 1985)

Bolles, Richard N., *The Three Boxes of Life* (Berkeley, CA: Ten Speed Press, 1981)

Crystal, John C. and Richard N. Bolles, *Where Do I Go From Here With My Life?* (Berkeley, CA: Ten Speed Press, 1979)

Edwards, Paul and Sarah, *Finding Your Perfect Work* (New York: Little, Brown, 1996)

Gale, Barry and Linda Gale, *Discover What You're Best At* (New York: Simon & Schuster, 1983)

Holland, John L., *Making Vocational Choices* (Englewood Cliffs, NJ: Prentice-Hall, 1985)

Krannich, Ronald L. and Caryl Rae, *Discover the Best Jobs For You!* (Manassas Park, VA: Impact Publications, 1998)

Miller, Arthur F. and Ralph T. Mattson, *The Truth About You: Discover What You Should Be Doing With Your Life* (Berkeley, CA: Ten Speed Press, 1989)

Sher, Barbara, *I Could Do Anything If Only I Knew What It Was* (New York: Ballantine, 1995)

Sher, Barbara, *Wishcraft* (New York: Ballantine, 1983)

Sturman, Gerald M., *Career Discovery Project* (New York: Bantam, 1992)

Tieger, Paul and Barbara Barron-Tieger, *Do What You Are* (New York: Little, Brown, 1995)

Research On Cities, Fields, and Organizations

Adams Media (ed.), *The Job Bank Series: Atlanta, Boston, Chicago, Dallas, Denver, Florida, Los Angeles, Minneapolis, New York, Ohio, Philadelphia, San Francisco, Seattle, Washington, DC* plus 25 other cities and states (Holbrook, MA: Adams Media, 1998)

Adams Media (ed.), *The National Job Bank* (Holbrook, MA: Adams Media, 1998)

Camden, Bishop, Schwartz, Greene, Fleming-Holland, *"How to Get a Job In..." Insider's City Guides: Atlanta, Chicago, New York, San Francisco, Seattle/Portland, Southern California* (Chicago, IL: Surrey, 1997-1998)

Hopke, William (ed.), *Encyclopedia of Careers and Vocational Guidance* (Chicago, IL: J. G. Ferguson, 1997)

Hoover, Gary, Alta Campbell, Patrick J. Spain, and Alan Chai (eds.), *Hoover's 500, Hoover's Handbook of World Business*, and *Hoover's Handbook of Emerging Companies* (Austin, TX: Reference Press, 1996-1997)

Krantz, Les, *Jobs Rated Almanac* (New York: Wiley, 1996)

Norback, Craig T., *Careers Encyclopedia* (Lincolnwood, IL: National Textbook, 1997)

Petras, Ross and Kathryn, *Jobs 1998* (New York: Simon & Schuster, 1997)

Schwartz, Lester and Irv Brechner, *The Career Finder* (New York: Ballantine, 1990)

U.S. Department of Labor, *The Dictionary of Occupational Titles* (Washington, DC: U.S. Department of Labor, 1991)

U.S. Department of Labor, *The Occupational Outlook Handbook* (Washington, DC: U.S. Department of Labor, 1998)

Wright, John W., *The American Almanac of Jobs and Salaries* (New York: Avon, 1996)

Resumes and Letters

Adams Media (ed.), *The Adams Resume Almanac* (Holbrook, MA: Adams Media, 1997)

Asher, Donald, *Asher's Bible of Executive Resumes* (Berkeley, CA: Ten Speed Press, 1996)

Beatty, Richard H., *175 High-Impact Resumes* (New York: Wiley, 1996)

Beatty, Richard H., *The Perfect Cover Letter* (New York: Wiley, 1997)

Bostwich, Burdette E., *Resume Writing* (New York: Wiley, 1995)

Corbin, Bill and Shelbi Wright, *The Edge Resume Job Search Strategy* (Indianapolis, IN: JIST Works, 1997)

Coxford, Lola M., *Resume Writing Made Easy* (Scottsdale, AZ: Gorsuch Scarisbrik, 1994)

Criscito, Pat, *Resumes in Cyberspace* (New York: Barrons, 1997)

Enelow, Wendy S., *100 Winning Resumes For $100,000+ Jobs* (Manassas Park, VA: Impact Publications, 1997)

Enelow, Wendy S., *1500+ KeyWords For $100,000+ Jobs* (Manassas Park, VA: Impact Publications, 1998)

Farr, Michael, *America's Top Resumes For America's Top Jobs* (Indianapolis, IN: JIST Works, 1997)

Fournier, Myra and Jeffrey Spin, *Encyclopedia of Job-Winning Resumes* (Richfield, CT: Round Lake Publishing, 1991)

Fry, Ronald, *Your First Resume* (Hawthorne, NJ: Career Press, 1995)

Good, C. Edward, *Does Your Resume Wear Blue Jeans?* (Charlottesville, VA: Blue Jeans Press, 1985)

Good, C. Edward, *Resumes For Re-Entry: A Woman's Handbook* (Manassas Park, VA: Impact Publications, 1993)

Jackson, Tom, *The New Perfect Resume* (New York: Doubleday, 1996)

Jackson, Tom, *Perfect Resume Strategies* (New York: Doubleday, 1992)

Kaplan, Robbie Miller, *101 Resumes For Sure-Hire Results* (New York: AMACOM, 1994)

Kaplan, Robbie Miller, *Resume Shortcuts* (Manassas Park, VA: Impact Publications, 1996)

Kaplan, Robbie Miller, *Sure-Hire Resumes* (Manassas Park, VA: Impact Publications, 1998)

Kennedy, Joyce Lain, *Resumes For Dummies* (Forest City, CA: IDG Books Worldwide, 1996)

Kennedy, Joyce Lain and Thomas J. Morrow, *Electronic Resume Revolution* (New York: Wiley, 1995)

Krannich, Ronald L. and Caryl Rae Krannich, *Dynamite Resumes* (Manassas Park, VA: Impact Publications, 1996)

Krannich, Ronald L. and William Banis, *High Impact Resumes and Letters* (Manassas Park, VA: Impact Publications, 1998)

Montag, Bill, *Best Resumes For $75,000+ Executive Jobs* (New York: Wiley, 1992)

Noble, David F., *The Gallery of Best Resumes* (Indianapolis, IN: JIST Works, 1994)

Parker, Yana, *The Damn Good Resume Guide* (Berkeley, NY: Ten Speed Press, 1996)

Parker, Yana, *The Resume Catalog* (Berkeley, NY: Ten Speed Press, 1996)

Swanson, David, *The Resume Solution* (Indianapolis, IN: JIST Works, 1995)

Weddle, Peter, *Internet Resumes* (Manassas Park, VA: Impact Publications, 1998)

Yate, Martin, *Resumes That Knock 'Em Dead* (Holbrook, MA: Adams Media, 1998)

Cover and Job Search Letters

Beatty, Richard H., *175 High-Impact Cover Letters* (New York: Wiley, 1996)

Beatty, Richard H., *Perfect Cover Letter* (New York: Wiley, 1997)

Fein, Richard, *Cover Letters! Cover Letters! Cover Letters!* (Hawthorne, NJ: Career Press, 1997)

Frank, William S., *200 Letters For Job Hunters* (Berkeley, CA: Ten Speed Press, 1995)

Kay, Andrea, *Covers Letters That Will Get You The Job You Want* (Cincinnati, OH: Betterway, 1996)

Kennedy, Joyce Lain, *Cover Letters For Dummies* (Forest City, CA: IDG Books Worldwide, 1996)

Krannich, Ronald L. and Caryl Rae Krannich, *201 Dynamite Job Search Letters* (Manassas Park, VA: Impact Publications, 1997)

Krannich, Ronald L. and Caryl Rae Krannich, *Dynamite Cover Letters* (Manassas Park, VA: Impact Publications, 1997)

Yate, Martin, *Cover Letters That Knock 'Em Dead* (Holbrook, MA: Adams Media, 1998)

Networking and Small Talk

Baber, Anne and Lynne Waymon, *Great Connections* (Manassas Park, VA: Impact Publications, 1993)

Beatty, Richard, *Richard Beatty's Job Search Networking* (Holbrook, MA: Adams Media, 1994)

Boe, Anne and Bettie B. Youngs, *Is Your "Net" Working?* (New York: Wiley, 1989)

Garnas, Les, *How to Use People and Get What You Want—and Still Be a Nice Guy!* (Princeton, NJ: Peterson's, 1994)

Krannich, Ronald L. and Caryl Rae Krannich, *Dynamite Networking For Dynamite Jobs* (Manassas, VA: Impact Publications, 1996)

Krannich, Ronald L. and Caryl Rae Krannich, *Dynamite Tele-Search* (Manassas, VA: Impact Publications, 1995)

Lowstuter, Clyde C. and David P. Robertson, *Network Your Way to Your Next Job* (New York: McGraw-Hill, 1994)

National Business Employment Week, *National Business Employment Weekly's Networking* (New York: Wiley, 1996)

RoAnn, Susan, *How to Work a Room* (New York: Warner Books, 1988)

RoAnn, Susan, *Secrets of Savvy Networking* (New York: Warner Books, 1992)

RoAnn, Susan, *What Do I Say Next?* (New York: Warner Books, 1997)

Tullier, L. Michelle, *Networking For Everyone* (Indianapolis: IN: JIST Works, 1998)

Vilas, Donna and Sanda, *Power Networking* (Austin, TX: Duke Publishing, 1992)

Dress, Appearance, and Image

Karpinski, Kenneth J., *Red Socks Don't Work: Messages from the Real Work About Men's Clothing* (Manassas Park, VA: Impact Publications, 1994)

Molloy, John T., *John Molloy's New Dress For Success* (New York: Warner Books, 1991)

Molloy, John T., *New Women's Dress For Success* (New York: Warner Books, 1997)

Nicholson, JoAnna, *110 Mistakes Working Women Make and How to Avoid Them: Dressing Smart For the '90s* (Manassas Park, VA: Impact Publications, 1994)

Interviews and Salary Negotiations

Beatty, R. H., *The Five Minute Interview* (New York: Wiley, 1986)

Chapman, Jack, *How to Make $1000 a Minute: Negotiating Salaries and Raises* (Berkeley, CA: Ten Speed Press, 1987)

Fry, Ronald, *101 Great Answers To the Toughest Interview Questions* (Hawthorne, NJ: Career Press, 1995)

Krannich, Caryl Rae and Ronald L. Krannich, *101 Dynamite Answers to Interview Questions* (Manassas Park, VA: Impact Publications, 1997)

Krannich, Caryl Rae and Ronald L. Krannich, *Interview For Success* (Manassas Park, VA: Impact Publications, 1998)

Krannich, Ronald L. and Caryl Rae Krannich, *Dynamite Salary Negotiations* (Manassas Park, VA: Impact Publications, 1998)

Medley, H. Anthony, *Sweaty Palms* (Berkeley, CA: Ten Speed Press, 1991)

Miller, Lee E., *Get More Money On Your Next Job* (New York: McGraw-Hill, 1997)

Simon, Mary B., *Negotiate Your Job Offer* (NewYork: Wiley, 1997)

Educators

Krannich, Ronald L. *Educator's Guide to Alternative Jobs and Careers* (Manassas Park, VA: Impact Publications, 1991)

Public-Oriented Careers

Damp, Dennis, *The Book of U.S. Government Jobs* (Corapolis, PA: D-Amp Publications, 1995)

Krannich, Ronald L. and Caryl Rae Krannich, *The Complete Guide to Public Employment* (Manassas Park, VA: Impact Publications, 1995)

Krannich, Ronald L. and Caryl Rae Krannich, *Directory of Federal Jobs and Employers* (Manassas Park, VA: Impact Publications, 1996)

Krannich, Ronald L. and Caryl Rae Krannich, *Find a Federal Job Fast!* (Manassas Park, VA: Impact Publications, 1998)

Krannich, Ronald L. and Caryl Rae Krannich, *Jobs and Careers With Nonprofit Organizations* (Manassas Park, VA: Impact Publications, 1998)

Lauber, Daniel, *The Government Job Finder* (River Forest, IL: Planning/Communications, 1997)

Lauber, Daniel, *The Nonprofit's and Education Job Finder* (River Forest, IL: Planning/Communication, 1997)

Smith, Russ, *Federal Applications That Get Results* (Manassas Park, VA: Impact Publications, 1996)

Smith, Russ, *Federal Jobs in Law Enforcement* (Manassas Park, VA: Impact Publications, 1996)

International and Overseas Jobs

Forbes, Moira, *Jobs in Russia and the Newly Independent States* (Manassas Park, VA: Impact Publications, 1994)

Foreign Policy Association (ed.), *Guide to Careers in World Affairs* (Manassas Park, VA: Impact Publications, 1993)

Kocher, Eric, *International Jobs* (Reading, MA: Addison-Wesley, 1993)

Krannich, Ronald L. and Caryl Rae Krannich, *The International Jobs Directory* (Manassas Park, VA: Impact Publications, 1998)

Krannich, Ronald L. and Caryl Rae Krannich, *The Complete Guide to International Jobs and Careers* (Manassas Park, VA: Impact Publications, 1993)

Krannich, Ronald L. and Caryl Rae Krannich, *Jobs For People Who Love Travel* (Manassas Park, VA: Impact Publications, 1995)

Lauber, Daniel, *International Job Finder* (River Forest, IL: Planning/ Communication, 1998)

Lay, David Caldwell and Benedict A. Leerburger, *Jobs Worldwide* (Manassas Park, VA: Impact Publications, 1996)

Military

Farley, Janet I., *Jobs and the Military Spouse* (Manassas Park, VA: Impact Publications, 1997)

Henderson, David G., *Job Search: Marketing Your Military Experience in the 1990s* (Harrisonburg, PA: Stackpole Books, 1995)

Jacobsen, Kenneth C., *Retiring From the Military* (Annapolis, MD: Naval Institute Press, 1994)

Savino, Carl and Ronald L. Krannich, *From Air Force Blue to Corporate Gray* (Manassas Park, VA: Impact Publications, 1996)

Savino, Carl and Ronald L. Krannich, *From Army Green to Corporate Gray* (Manassas Park, VA: Impact Publications, 1997)

Savino, Carl and Ronald L. Krannich, *From Navy Blue to Corporate Gray* (Manassas Park, VA: Impact Publications, 1995)

Savino, Carl and Ronald L. Krannich, *Resumes and Job Search Letters For Transitioning Military Personnel* (Manassas Park, VA: Impact Publications, 1997)

Women and Spouses

Bastress, Fran, *The New Relocating Spouse's Guide to Employment* (Manassas Park, VA: Impact Publications, 1993)

Martin, Renee and Don, *A Survival Guide For Women* (Washington, DC: Regnery Gateway, 1991)

College Students

Bouchard, Jerry, *Graduating to the 9-5 World* (Manassas Park, VA: Impact Publications, 1991)

Krueger, Brian D., *College Grad Job Hunter* (Holbrook, MA: Adams Media, 1998)

LaFevre, John L., *How You Really Get Hired* (New York: Simon & Schuster, 1994)

Minorities and Special Needs Groups

Johnson, Willis L. (ed.), *The Big Book of Minority Group Members* (Garrett Park, MD: Garrett Park Press, 1995)

Kastre, Michael, Alfred Edwards, and Nydia Rodriguez Kastre, *Minority Career Guide* (Princeton, NJ: Peterson's, 1993)

Kissane, Sharon F., *Career Success For People With Physical Disabilities* (Lincolnwood, IL: NTC Publishing, 1996)

Rivera, Miquela, *The Minority Career Handbook* (Holbrook, MA: Adams Media, 1990)

Witt, Melanie Astaire, *Job Strategies For People With Disabilities* (Princeton, NJ: Peterson's, 1992)

Alternative Career Fields

Basta, Nick, *Careers in High Tech* (Lincolnwood, IL: NTC Publishing, 1992)

Edelfedt, Roy A., *Careers in Education* (Lincolnwood, IL: NTC Publishing, 1993)

Field, Shelly, *100 Best Careers in Casinos and Casino Hotels* (New York: Arco, 1996)

Hiam, Alex and Susan Angle, *Adventure Careers* (Hawthorne, NJ: Career Press, 1995)

Krannich, Ronald L. and Caryl Rae Krannich, *Best Jobs For the 21st Century* (Manassas Park, VA: Impact Publications, 199)

Mantis, Hillary and Kathleen Brady, *Jobs For Lawyers* (Manassas Park, VA: Impact Publications, 1996)

"Opportunities In..." Career Series (180 titles), (Lincolnwood, IL: NTC Publishing, 1990-1998)

Peterson's (ed.), *Job Opportunities in Health Care* (Princeton, NJ: Peterson's, 1997)

Rubin, K., *Flying High In Travel: A Complete Guide to Careers in the Travel Industry* (New York: Wiley, 1992)

Shenk, Ellen, *Outdoor Careers* (Harrisonburg, PA: Stackpole Books, 1992)

Stair, Lila B., *Careers in Computers* (Lincolnwood, IL: NTC Publishing, 1995)

CD-ROM Programs

Ace the Interview (Charleston, WV: Cambridge Career Products, 1997)

Adams JobBank Fast Resume (Holbrook, MA: Adams Media, 1996)

Electronic Enhanced Dictionary of Occupational Titles (Indianapolis, IN: JIST Works, 1996)

The Encyclopedia of Careers and Vocational Guidance (Chicago: Ferguson, 1997)

Job Search Skills For the 21st Century (Vancouver, WA: The School Company, 1996)

JobBrowser Pro (Spokane, WA: JobQuest, 1997)

Multimedia Career Center (Charleston, WV: Cambridge Career Products, 1994)

The Ultimate Job Source (Orem, UT: InfoBusiness, 1995)

What Color Is Your Parachute? (Bubblebee Technology, 1997)

Win-Way Resumes 4.0 (Sacramento, CA: Win-Way, 1996)

The Authors

Caryl Rae Krannich, Ph.D., and Ronald L. Krannich, Ph.D., operate Development Concepts Inc., a training, consulting, and publishing firm. Caryl received her Ph.D. in Speech Communication from Penn State University. Ron received his Ph.D. in Political Science from Northern Illinois University.

Caryl and Ron are former university professors, high school teachers, management trainers, and consultants. They have completed numerous projects on management, career development, local government, population planning, and rural development during the past twenty years.

In addition to their extensive public sector work, the Krannichs are two of America's leading career and travel writers. They are authors of 28 career books and 11 travel books. Their career books focus on key job search skills, government jobs, international careers, nonprofit organizations, and career transitions. Their work represents one of today's most extensive and highly praised collections of career writing: *101 Dynamite Answers to Interview Questions, 101 Secrets of Highly Effective Speakers, 201 Dynamite Job Search Letters, Best Jobs For the 21st Century, Change Your Job Change Your Life, The Complete Guide to International Jobs and Careers, Discover the Best Jobs For You, Dynamite Cover Letters, Dynamite Resumes, Dynamite Salary Negotiations, Dynamite Tele-Search, The Educator's Guide to Alternative Jobs and Careers, Find a Federal Job Fast, From Air Force Blue to Corporate Gray, From Army Green to Corporate Gray, From Navy Blue to Corporate Gray, Resumes and Job Search Letters For Transitioning Military Personnel, High Impact Resumes and Letters, International Jobs Directory, Interview For Success, Jobs and Careers With Nonprofit Organizations, Jobs For People Who Love Travel,* and *Dynamite Networking For Dynamite Jobs.* Their books are found in most bookstores, libraries, and career centers. Many of their works are now available interactively on CD-ROM (*The Ultimate Job Source*).

Ron and Caryl continue to pursue their international interests through their innovative *"Treasures and Pleasures...Best of the Best"* travel series. When they are not found at their home and business in Virginia, they are probably somewhere in Europe, Asia, Africa, the Middle East, the South Pacific, or the Caribbean pursuing their other passion—researching and writing about quality arts and antiques.

Index

Career Resources

C ontact Impact Publications for a free annotated listing of career resources or visit their World Wide Web site for a complete listing of career resources: *http://www.impactpublications.com*. The following career resources, many of which were mentioned in previous chapters, are available directly from Impact Publications. Complete the following form or list the titles, include postage (see formula at the end), enclose payment, and send your order to:

IMPACT PUBLICATIONS
9104-N Manassas Drive
Manassas Park, VA 20111-5211
1-800-361-1055 (orders only)
Tel. 703/361-7300 or Fax 703/335-9486
E-mail address: *impactp@impactpublications.com*

Orders from individuals must be prepaid by check, moneyorder, Visa, MasterCard, or American Express. We accept telephone and fax orders.

Qty.	TITLES	Price	TOTAL

INTERVIEWS, NETWORKING & SALARY NEGOTIATIONS

Qty.	TITLES	Price	TOTAL
___	90-Minute Interview Prep Book	$15.95	___
___	101 Dynamite Answers to Interview Questions	$12.95	___
___	101 Dynamite Questions to Ask At Your Job Interview	$14.95	___
___	111 Dynamite Ways to Ace Your Job Interview	$13.95	___
___	201 Answers to the Toughest Job Interview Questions	$10.95	___
___	Adams Job Interview Almanac	$10.95	___
___	Best Answers to 201 Most Frequently Asked Interview Questions	$10.95	___
___	Dynamite Networking For Dynamite Jobs	$15.95	___

__ Dynamite Salary Negotiation	$15.95	_____
__ Get More Money On Your Next Job	$14.95	_____
__ Great Connections	$19.95	_____
__ How to Work a Room	$9.95	_____
__ Interview For Success	$15.95	_____
__ Interview Kit	$10.95	_____
__ Interview Power	$12.95	_____
__ Job Interviews For Dummies	$12.99	_____
__ NBEW's Interviewing	$11.95	_____
__ Negotiate Your Job Offer	$14.95	_____
__ Power Schmoozing	$12.95	_____
__ Quick Interview and Salary Negotiation Book	$12.95	_____
__ The Secrets of Savvy Networking	$11.99	_____
__ Sweaty Palms	$8.95	_____
__ What Do I Say Next?	$20.00	_____

COVER LETTERS

__ 175 High-Impact Cover Letters	$10.95	_____
__ 200 Letters For Job Hunters	$19.95	_____
__ 201 Dynamite Job Search Letters	$19.95	_____
__ 201 Killer Cover Letters	$16.95	_____
__ 201 Winning Cover Letters For $100,000+ Jobs	$24.95	_____
__ Adams Cover Letter Almanac and Disk	$19.95	_____
__ Cover Letters For Dummies	$12.99	_____
__ Cover Letters That Knock 'Em Dead	$10.95	_____
__ Dynamite Cover Letters	$14.95	_____
__ NBEW's Cover Letters	$11.95	_____
__ Perfect Cover Letter	$10.95	_____
__ Sure-Hire Cover Letters	$10.95	_____

RÉSUMÉS

__ 101 Great Résumés	$9.99	_____
__ 101 Résumés For Sure-Hire Results	$10.95	_____
__ 175 High-Impact Résumés	$10.95	_____
__ 201 Winning Resumes For $100,000+ Jobs	$24.95	_____
__ 1500+ KeyWords For $100,000+ Jobs	$14.95	_____
__ Adams Résumé Almanac	$10.95	_____
__ Asher's Bible of Executive Résumés	$29.95	_____
__ Best Résumés For $75,000+ Executive Jobs	$14.95	_____
__ Complete Idiot's Guide to Crafting the Perfect Résumé	$16.95	_____
__ Designing the Perfect Résumé	$12.95	_____
__ Dynamite Résumés	$14.95	_____
__ Electronic Résumé Revolution	$12.95	_____
__ Electronic Résumés: Putting Your Résumé On-Line	$19.95	_____
__ Electronic Résumés For the New Job Market	$11.95	_____
__ Encyclopedia of Job-Winning Résumés	$16.95	_____
__ Gallery of Best Résumés	$16.95	_____
__ Gallery of Best Résumés For Two-Year Degree Graduates	$14.95	_____
__ High Impact Résumés and Letters	$14.95	_____
__ How to Prepare Your Curriculum Vitae	$14.95	_____
__ Internet Resumes	$14.95	_____

__ NBEW's Résumés	$11.95	_____
__ New Perfect Résumé	$10.95	_____
__ Power Résumés	$12.95	_____
__ Real-Life Résumés That Work!	$12.95	_____
__ Résumé Catalog	$15.95	_____
__ Résumé Pro	$24.95	_____
__ Résumé Shortcuts	$14.95	_____
__ Résumé Solution	$12.95	_____
__ Résumés For Advertising Careers	$9.95	_____
__ Résumés For Architecture and Related Careers	$9.95	_____
__ Résumés For Banking and Financial Careers	$9.95	_____
__ Résumés For Business Management Careers	$9.95	_____
__ Résumés For College Students and Recent Graduates	$9.95	_____
__ Résumés For Communications Careers	$9.95	_____
__ Résumés For Dummies	$12.99	_____
__ Résumés For Education Careers	$9.95	_____
__ Résumés For Engineering Careers	$9.95	_____
__ Résumés For Environmental Careers	$9.95	_____
__ Résumés For 50+ Job Hunters	$9.95	_____
__ Résumés For First-Time Job Hunter	$9.95	_____
__ Résumés For the Healthcare Professional	$12.95	_____
__ Résumés For High School Graduates	$9.95	_____
__ Résumés For High Tech Careers	$9.95	_____
__ Résumés For Midcareer Job Changers	$9.95	_____
__ Résumés For the Over 50 Job Hunter	$14.95	_____
__ Résumés For Re-Entering the Job Market	$9.95	_____
__ Résumés For Sales and Marketing Careers	$9.95	_____
__ Résumés For Scientific and Technical Careers	$9.95	_____
__ Résumés That Knock 'Em Dead	$10.95	_____
__ Résumés, Résumés, Résumés	$9.99	_____
__ Sure-Hire Résumés	$14.95	_____

SKILLS, TESTING, SELF-ASSESSMENT, EMPOWERMENT

__ 7 Habits of Highly Effective People	$14.00	_____
__ Career Satisfaction and Success	$9.95	_____
__ Chicken Soup For the Soul	$12.95	_____
__ Discover the Best Jobs For You	$14.95	_____
__ Do What You Are	$14.95	_____
__ Do What You Love, the Money Will Follow	$10.95	_____
__ I Can Do Anything If Only I Knew What It Was	$19.95	_____
__ Love Your Work and Success Will Follow	$12.95	_____
__ P.I.E. Method For Career Success	$14.95	_____
__ Seven Habits of Highly Effective People	$14.00	_____
__ Your Signature Path	$24.95	_____

JOB SEARCH STRATEGIES AND TACTICS

__ 101 Great Answers to the Toughest Job Search Problems	$11.99	_____
__ 110 Biggest Mistakes Job Hunters Make	$19.95	_____
__ 303 Off the Wall Ways to Get a Job	$12.99	_____
__ Change Your Job, Change Your Life	$17.95	_____
__ Complete Job Finder's Guide to the 90s	$13.95	_____

__ Dynamite Tele-Search	$12.95	_____
__ Five Secrets to Finding a Job	$12.95	_____
__ How to Get Interviews From Classified Job Ads	$14.95	_____
__ Job Hunter's Catalog	$10.95	_____
__ Job Hunting For Dummies	$16.99	_____
__ Joyce Lain Kennedy's Career Book	$29.95	_____
__ Knock 'Em Dead	$12.95	_____
__ Me, Myself, and I, Inc	$17.95	_____
__ New Rites of Passage At $100,000+	$29.95	_____
__ Professional's Private Sector Job Finder	$18.95	_____
__ What Color Is Your Parachute?	$16.95	_____

SUBTOTAL   _____

Virginia residents add 4½% sales tax   _____

POSTAGE/HANDLING ($5.00 for first
title plus 8% of SUBTOTAL over $30) $5.00

8% of SUBTOTAL over $30----------------------- _____

TOTAL ENCLOSED ------------------- _____

SHIP TO:

NAME _____

ADDRESS _____

_____

❑ I enclose check/moneyorder for $ _____ made payable to
IMPACT PUBLICATIONS.

❑ Please charge $ _____ to my credit card:

❑ Visa   ❑ MasterCard   ❑ American Express

Card # _____

Expiration date: _____/_____

Signature _____

We accept official purchase orders from libraries, educational institutions, and
government offices. Please attach copy with official signature(s).

The On-Line Superstore & Warehouse

Hundreds of Terrific Career Resources Conveniently Available
On the World V

65 Days a Year!

Ever wanted to know what are the newest and best books, directories, newsletters, wall charts, training programs, videos, CD-ROMs, computer software, and kits available to help you land a job, negotiate a higher salary, or start your own business? What about finding a job in Asia or relocating to San Francisco? Are you curious about how to find a job 24-hours a day by using the Internet or what you'll be doing five years from now? Trying to keep up-to-date on the latest career resources but not able to find the latest catalogs, brochures, or newsletters on today's "best of the best" resources?

Welcome to the first virtual career bookstore on the Internet. Now you're only a "click" away with Impact Publication's electronic solution to the resource challenge. Impact Publications, one of the nation's leading publishers and distributors of career resources, has launched its comprehensive "Career Superstore and Warehouse" on the Internet. The bookstore is jam-packed with the latest job and career resources on:

- Alternative jobs and careers
- Self-assessment
- Career planning and job search
- Employers
- Relocation and cities
- Resumes
- Cover Letters
- Dress, image, and etiquette
- Education
- Telephone
- Military
- Salaries
- Interviewing
- Nonprofits

- Empowerment
- Self-esteem
- Goal setting
- Executive recruiters
- Entrepreneurship
- Government
- Networking
- Electronic job search
- International jobs
- Travel
- Law
- Training and presentations
- Minorities
- Physically challenged

The bookstore also includes a new "Military Career Transition Center" and "School-to-Work Center."

"This is more than just a bookstore offering lots of product," say Drs. Ron and Caryl Krannich, two of the nation's leading career experts and authors and developers of this on-line bookstore. *"We're an important resource center for libraries, corporations, government, educators, trainers, and career counselors who are constantly defining and redefining this dynamic field. Of the thousands of career resources we review each year, we only select the 'best of the best.'"*

Visit this rich site and you'll quickly discover just about everything you ever wanted to know about finding jobs, changing careers, and starting your own business—including many useful resources that are difficult to find in local bookstores and libraries. The site also includes what's new and hot, tips for job search success, and monthly specials. Impact's Web address is:

http://www.impactpublications.com